SILVERSMITHING
A Manual of Design and Techniques

SILVERSMITHING
A Manual of Design and Techniques

Keith Smith

The Crowood Press

First published in 2000 by
The Crowood Press Ltd
Ramsbury, Marlborough
Wiltshire SN8 2HR

British Library Cataloguing in Publication Data
A catalogue record for this book is available from the British Library.

ISBN 1 86126 318 X

Acknowledgements
The Hallmarks data sheet on p.151 is reproduced with the kind permission of the
Assay Offices of the United Kingdom.

Typeset by Phoenix Typesetting
Ilkley, West Yorkshire.

Printed and bound in Great Britain by
T. J. International, Padstow.

Contents

Introduction

The craft of the silversmith has changed little over the centuries, apart from the introduction of such equipment as gas torches, electric polishing motors and lathes, which either speed up production or make life easier.

It is difficult to select any one period in the craft as especially outstanding. One only has to look at an Etruscan gold bowl made in or around 600BC, with decoration formed from 137,000 gold grains and with designed and flattering repoussé decoration to realize that clever and beautiful things have been made in every era. The choice of a period regarded as outstanding is a personal matter, and often relates to a loyalty for a style or a fashion, such as the Adam period, for instance.

There are many people who believe that nothing that is contemporary is of any worth, but this is often nostalgic nonsense. New styles have probably always been condemned, but nothing is surer than that the best of the work of today's silversmiths will be revered and collected in the future.

The craft may be practised in the most modest of circumstances, as well as in lavishly equipped workshops. There are many designer silversmiths who work at home, either within their houses or in outhouses or sheds in the garden. It is not unknown for someone to undertake quiet activities such as filing and fitting in the house, to do the hammering in a shed at the bottom of the garden, to heat and solder the metal in the coalhouse, and to polish the work in the garage.

Home silversmiths often work in very small workshops; the author is able to make and solder large pieces in a workshop measuring 2.5m (8ft 3in) long by 1.75m (5ft 10in) wide, with a bench 1.5m (59in) long by 57cm (22.5in) wide. Of course, others may have much larger workshops and design studios, but those who wish to practise for leisure or business should not be discouraged by their less than ideal circumstances.

Anyone working from home should carefully consider his or her household insurance liabilities, even more so if a business enterprise is to be considered, and in such circumstances business rates and planning permission may also be involved. In relation to insurance liability it is absolutely essential that safety matters are given the greatest consideration so that cover is not endangered.

Group workshops are also available for silversmiths in a variety of situations, such as craft centres, old commercial premises or council-sponsored units. Local area Arts Boards or a search through crafts magazines may reveal the locations of group workshops. Obviously a group workshop enables an economical pooling of resources for anyone in, or starting a business enterprise.

Finally, all the techniques that are described in the ensuing chapters were learned during my early training and subsequent practice as a teacher and designer craftsman. I have also read of the work of others and learned much as a result of working with a number of experts. As a result I have learned that there is often more than one way of doing most things, and, even if you accept my instructions to the very last word, with practice you will certainly develop your own variations and may even become an innovator in some area.

— 2 —

The Workshop

This chapter describes the very basic hardware and materials that are used whatever the technique you are involved in. Detailed descriptions of all specialist tools are to be found in the chapters to which they apply; hence raising hammers are described in the chapter on raising, as are raising stakes.

THE BENCH

It is true to say that while the simplest leisure activities, such as the production of small dishes, napkin rings and small spoons, have often been undertaken on the proverbial kitchen table anything more ambitious requires a sturdy bench.

The ideal bench will have a working surface of beech wood 50mm (2in) thick and will have softwood legs 50mm (2in) by 90mm (3.5in). The total height of the bench should be approximately 900mm (36in). At each end of the bench the legs should be cross-braced and diagonally braced at the back so as to eliminate excessive wobbling when a vice is tightened or loosened, or when heavy hammering is undertaken. At a convenient point there should be a curved cut-out on the front edge of the bench. This cut-out allows you to sit and work with tools within easy reach. A leather or plastic apron may be nailed around the underside of the cut-out to catch precious metal filings and clippings. It will also catch dropped work and tools.

In the centre of the cut-out a deep slot should be cut. Into this slot fits a bench pin that you can easily make for yourself. The bench pin is a flat, rectangular piece of hardwood with a vee cut out at one end and a tongue at the other end; this fits into the slot in the bench. With the tongue pushed into the bench slot, the bench pin projects towards you and may be turned over to provide two working modes. The tongue is cut in such a way that the surface of the pin may either be flush with the bench top to aid saw piercing, or turned over to aid filing on a surface which is lower than the bench top and that has been cut to a slope. The pin may be cut and notched in a variety of ways to aid the holding of work while it is being filed. It is easily made, quite expendable, but a particularly valuable piece of equipment.

Although it has been stated that the ideal bench top should be of hardwood, this is an expensive option and suitable material may be difficult to obtain. The author has constructed a worktop of planed softwood

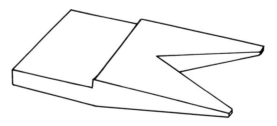

Bench pin.

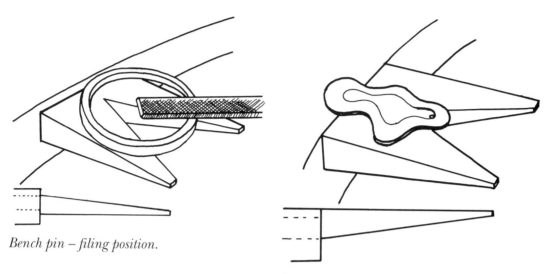

Bench pin – filing position.

Bench pin – piercing position.

of the sort that may be obtained from any good, local, wood yard or DIY. store. It is made from lengths of wood 100mm (4in) wide and 50mm (2in) thick, progressively glued and screwed edge to edge until the required width was achieved. Kitchen worktop or medium-density fibreboard are not suitable: the longitudinal strength of wood grain is essential.

THE BENCH VICE

A good quality, heavy, engineer's vice is essential and it should be fastened to the bench with strong bolts and as near to a bench leg as possible. This position for the vice is essential, so that when hammering is undertaken the force and the effect of the blows are not dissipated because of a vibrating and less than firm support. The cost of a new vice is surprisingly reasonable; but, of course, it is always possible to obtain a used and thus cheaper model in a saleroom or secondhand shop.

GAS SUPPLY, TORCHES AND THE HEARTH

A survey of designer silversmiths suggests that most of those who work at home use a bottled gas supply, while most of those who work in group workshops have a natural gas supply. The choice of supply is probably mainly a matter of cost and convenience. To lay on a supply of natural gas to a workshop at home may be costly and difficult, whereas group workshops in old commercial premises will probably have had the service installed at some time in the past. Of course, if a home workshop has a dual purpose then gas bottles are easily removed.

Natural gas has to be mixed with air blown from a rotary blower or compressor, and it is also possible to do the same with bottled gas. The advantage of blown air is that a very hot flame of varying length may easily be achieved with a torch with a large nozzle, allowing convenient operations on workpieces large and small. With unblown bottled gas it really is necessary to change nozzles according to the size of the piece of work that is being heated. The versatility of the torch with blown air may be much preferred for soldering operations where a work piece may be swiftly heated with a large flame, which may then be reduced in size and concentrated upon the area to be soldered. This can reduce the risk that joints that have already been made may be melted, and it is also easier to apply the solder in strip or rod form where there is not a great surrounding area of extreme heat.

Gas and air torches for natural and bottled gas appear to be identical, so it is essential to identify precisely the model that you are purchasing.

Torches for use with bottled gas, and without a blown air supply, achieve a long and very hot flame by drawing air into the flame through holes in the nozzle heads. As has already been indicated, it is not possible to produce a wide variety of flame sizes with one large nozzle and thus it is necessary to possess a range of sizes. The majority of designer makers produce a variety of wares large and small and so tend to have as many as four different nozzles. The nozzles fit to a torch by screw threads and are easily changed. Some people have two torches attached to the same gas bottle, with differently sized nozzles, so as to lessen the need to change nozzles. It is most important to choose the correct nozzle for the job in hand. It is a complete waste of time to use a small nozzle which will never achieve the heat that is required, and even to use one which will achieve the required heat, but over an absurd length of time, will only cause a damaging build up of dirty oxides on the surface of the metal. This would be particularly detrimental if a soldering operation were involved.

THE HEARTH

If work is to be heated to high temperatures and with large flames it must necessarily be done on a suitable hearth. The hearth will need to be revolved by hand while the heating takes place so that the work may be heated evenly and so that all-round soldering operations may be undertaken. A revolving hearth may be obtained from a silversmiths' tool-shop, or you may be able to instruct a local sheet-metal worker or engineer to make one for you. For reasons of fire safety the hearth should stand on a steel table, and the local ironmonger, DIY stores, or a scrapyard may provide the materials to make one for yourself. The top surface could be insulated with mill-board, which is a modern, safe substitute for asbestos. *Under no circumstances should old asbestos be used.*

The hearth should be filled with a large firebrick, or refractory bricks, on which work that is to be heated can be placed. Ideally, you should have a collection of bricks of several sizes so that work may be propped and supported at any angle. If possible, the hearth should be placed in the darkest corner of the workshop so that when heating and soldering takes place it is easy to see when the metal is approaching red heat. It would be desirable, but may be considered a luxury, if the hearth could be topped by a canopy with an extractor fan to remove excessive fumes.

PICKLE AND SULPHURIC ACID

Metal that has been heated is dirty and oxidized and, if soldering has taken place, will bear traces of glassy borax. The metal is cleaned by immersing it in a pickle, which may be hot or cold, the former producing the faster result.

Pickle may take the form of dilute sulphuric acid, a 'safety pickle' (sodium bisulphate) or alum. A survey of designer silversmiths suggests that a majority of those who work at home use safety pickle. Safety pickle is sold as fine crystals, is not corrosive until it is wet and is therefore easier and safer to transport to the workshop than a glass container of acid. Furthermore, it is sold in precise quantities, in sealed bags, to make convenient quantities of liquid, therefore eliminating the need to store dangerous corrosives. Instructions are enclosed with packs of safety pickle and they should be followed precisely; the attendant dangers should be carefully noted.

Sulphuric acid is the preferred pickle of the majority of those who work in group workshops. It must be diluted to the proportion of one part of acid to nine or ten of water. In mixing an acid pickle it is essential to add the acid slowly to the required quantity of water, stirring the solution, which will become warm, all the time. *You must never add water to acid, to do so is dangerous and may result in an explosion.*

Pickle is perfectly effective as a cold solution but it takes time to work; if it is warmed it will be much quicker in its action. Silversmiths' shops sell polypropylene pickle tanks fitted with thermostatically-controlled heaters. Pickle solutions do, of course, evaporate and they should be topped up a little and often. Hot metals should not be plunged direct into pickle because of the risk of dangerous splashing and the generation of choking fumes.

TONGS AND TWEEZERS

If hot silver or gold is to be handled and if, when cold, it is to be immersed in or removed from pickle then long-handled tongs are required. They may be made of brass, copper or nickel silver, but not of iron or steel. If silver is held in iron tongs and immersed in pickle a chemical change takes place and a coating of copper is deposited upon the silver, and the pickle is spoilt.

A pair of strong iron or steel tongs is extremely useful for holding hot iron or steel during forging operations. Many useful tools may be made by using simple forging techniques, probably with inexpensive materials from the local scrap yard. Iron or steel tongs may often be found in tool sales.

Two or three pairs of tweezers are also useful in the workshop. It is worth buying a good quality pair in stainless steel, with fine accurate points, so that small pieces of solder may be picked up and placed where they are needed. For removing extremely small items from a pickle basket a pair of brass tweezers may also be useful.

POLISHING EQUIPMENT

Although there are people who polish their work only by hand, the majority use an electric polishing motor, with a tapered and threaded spindle on each side. It is sometimes awkward to polish pieces on only one side of the motor and, of course, two spindles will allow two people to work at the same time. The polishing motor must be bolted to a strong bench, and it is possible, although costly, to obtain purpose-built benches with hoods and dust extractors. Dust hoods without extractors are also available and confine the spread of dust reasonably. It should also be perfectly feasible for you to make your own dust hood using sheet metal or plywood. Tool shops and shops specializing in safety equipment sell polycarbonate safety spectacles and simple dust masks, enabling you to work within the health and safety rules. A board on which polishing mops may be hung should also be made, so that the mops do not lie in dirt and dust which may be picked up, only to damage the work to be polished. The several types of mop and their use are described in Chapter 14 on finishing and polishing.

THE STORAGE OF TOOLS

The careful storage of tools is of paramount importance. The craft of the silversmith involves much hammering of a soft and precious metal over hard steel stakes. If the hammer faces are cut and damaged and the stakes are in a similar condition then, after working, the precious metal will be covered with replicas of the damaged surfaces. Removing the marks involves a great waste of metal and time and an all-round expense. It follows, therefore, that simple racks and storage beds should be made for all hammers and stakes. Files are also damaged and blunted if they are piled in a box or drawer, and shuffling them about to find the one that you want causes most of the damage. Once again racks are easily made from scrap wood. For sheer convenience pliers and saws should also have somewhere to hang. There is nothing more infuriating than having to search through a pile of tools for the one that you particularly wish to use. Discipline is everything!

— 3 —

Metals

There is a variety of metals that may be used by anyone who wishes to use silver-smithing techniques. As we point out later, non-precious metals are actually more difficult to obtain in small quantities than are precious metals. The essential qualities of useful metals are listed below.

COPPER

Copper has a melting point of 1,083°C, an attractive colour and is soft and therefore easy to work. Because it is soft, it is easily damaged in storage and in working, and it is a tedious business to bring it back to a flawless finish. It acquires a fine, soft polish after years of hand polishing. It should be annealed by heating to a red heat and quenching in water.

BRASS

Brass consists of 70 per cent copper and 30 per cent zinc, has a melting point of 1,015°C and is a very hard material suitable for turning and spinning. Because of its yellow colour it may have uses in metal lamination work in non-assayable pieces. It is not good for soldering at very high temperatures since it has a tendency to collapse suddenly. It is to hard to raise and tends to warp in sheet form.

GILDING METAL

Gilding metal consists of 85 per cent copper and 15 per cent zinc and strikes a balance between the hardness of brass and the softness of copper. It takes a much better finish than copper and does not collapse nor warp under heat like brass. It is the best all-purpose metal for anyone who does not want or cannot afford to use silver. It should be annealed by heating it to red heat and quenching it in cold water.

SILVER

Silver is obviously the silversmith's metal and it is produced in four hallmarking quality alloys. Three of these have been commonly in use in the United Kingdom for a considerable length of time and have been known as standard or sterling silver, Britannia silver and enamelling silver. A new type was introduced on 1 January 1999 known as 800 grade.

Silver is as close to a perfect metal for the silversmith as it is possible to get, and with skill and care, and the correct alloy, there is almost nothing that cannot be achieved, such is its ductility and versatility. The four alloys are described below.

STANDARD OR STERLING SILVER

This is now also known as 925, consisting of 925 parts silver and 75 parts copper, with a melting point of 890°C. This is the alloy for general silversmithing, being suitable for raising, forging, and repoussé and other demanding techniques. It is generally annealed by heating to red heat and quenching in cold water. Heating standard silver with a gas torch causes the copper in the alloy to oxidize on the surface as a grey skin which is known as 'firestain'. How to deal with firestain is explained in Chapter 14. There is continuing research on the production of a fire-free alloy and you should enquire about the availability of such an alloy from your bullion dealer.

BRITANNIA SILVER

This is also known as 958 and consists of 958 parts silver and 42 parts copper, with a melting point 920°C. The alloy was originally introduced in 1697 when silver coinage was of the 925 standard and silversmiths were clipping the edges of coins to obtain free silver to make their wares. Between 1697 and 1719 all silver plate had to be of the Britannia standard. The standard has remained an option, although it is a very soft alloy and needs to be used in a heavy gauge.

ENAMELLING SILVER

This is alternatively known as 999. As suggested by its name, the alloy is usually used in conjunction with vitreous enamels. Other alloys produce firestain that endangers the adherence of the enamel to the metal.

800 SILVER

This was introduced as an alloy that may be hallmarked in the United Kingdom from the beginning of 1999. It is an alloy commonly used in mainland Europe, but for the designer craftsman it may not be an ideal one. With a silver content of 800 parts to 200 parts of mainly copper, the problems of dealing with very heavy firestain may be insurmountable. If there are any savings in the costs of metal these could quickly be lost in the inflated working costs. Clearly designers and craftsmen must decide for themselves, but it would seem to be advisable to begin with only small, experimental pieces.

GOLD

You may wish to apply or inlay small amounts of gold to your silver, or you could conceivably be asked to make something in gold! There are six grades available and in a variety of colours including white, yellow, red and green. Obviously you would not want to use white gold with silver, but the only other reservations will be the working nature of the alloys. Nine carat gold, or 375, has only little gold in the alloy, 375 parts in 1,000, and its working characteristics and colour are not ideal; 585 or fourteen carat is better, but the best as regards colour, working and reasonable hardness is 750, or eighteen carat; 750 is reasonable as an applied material such as wire or shot. If you wished to inlay into an undercut channel, then something like 990 or 999 might be used.

NICKEL SILVER

A grey metal comprising nickel, copper, and zinc in various proportions. It is a very hard material that has been used extensively by the trade, and finished by silverplating, hence the acronym EPNS (electrolplated nickel silver). If it is available it would be suitable for the production of dishes and cylindrical boxes. It is a good material for industrial spinning and stamping, but impossible for hand raising.

LEAD

Lead, with a melting point of 327°C, may be useful as a material in which to make simple moulds for stamping spoon bowls. It can be a dangerous material on account of its low melting point, and if it is not handled with care it can easily spill and splash when it is molten. The fumes are also dangerous and so it should be worked only in a well ventilated space, preferably in the open air. You must scrub your hands immediately after handling it. Do not allow children to handle it since it is poisonous.

— 4 —

Health and Safety

Serious health and safety warnings are included in this book in all the appropriate chapters, and in relation to particular techniques. Health and safety is an important matter and you ignore the advice and warnings that are offered here at your own risk; it will therefore be your own responsibility if any injuries are suffered. Always remember that in relation to the use of machinery and the handling of dangerous substances the old saying that familiarity breeds contempt is most apt. The main areas of concern for a silversmith are dealt with below.

ACIDS, PICKLES, ETCHING AGENTS AND OTHER CORROSIVE LIQUIDS

Any such liquids and agents must be used in the manner as laid down by the manufacturers. In use they should be stored and used in containers recommended by retailers and manufacturers. Durable polypropylene tanks are available for holding pickle. Do not use any home-made or botched-up heating system for acids or pickles; there are heating tanks available from silversmiths' tool shops, and if anything goes wrong the manufacturer is responsible.

Always keep pickles and corrosive liquids at the back of the bench or in a fume cupboard and obviously well out of the reach of children.

Use brass tongs and rubber gloves for handling work that has been removed from pickle for inspection or for washing. Never plunge hot metal into acid or pickle and, if there is any danger of liquid splashing, wear safety spectacles or a visor.

FLAMES

The dangers of fire may seem obvious, but it is worth making some comment on them, particularly for those who work from home and perhaps in a less than ideal environment.

Make sure that your hearth does not have inflammable debris around it and clear it up regularly. Do not hang a burning torch on the hearth while you do something else. If you use bottled gas close all the taps back to the bottle after use. If you work at home store your matches away when you are not working.

PITCH

The dangers involved in the use of pitch are carefully dealt with in Chapter 13 on decoration. Hot pitch is dangerous and if it adheres to your skin a serious burn will result. If you pour it from a two-handled container, use heavy industrial gloves and work in a well ventilated area. It is safer not to pour it but rather to break off lumps from your store block, place them where you want them and heat them there. Do not push hot pitch around with a wet thumb, use a cold planishing stake.

MOVING MACHINERY

Obviously you must take great care when using high-speed machinery, but once again familiarity often breeds contempt and many people indulge in incredibly dangerous practices. Moving machinery includes polishing motors and grindstones, vertical drills, sanding or linishing machines, lathes and milling machines.

In the use of all moving machinery loose clothing must not be worn, and long hair must be tied back, covered with a hat or held in place by a close-fitting collar or a high-necked garment. Not even the smallest wisp should be allowed to fall free.

In the case of vertical drills, milling machines and lathes any transparent safety guards must be used. They not only prevent the danger that hair or clothing might catch in moving chucks and cutters, but protect you from flying fragments of the material that is being worked.

In using all moving machinery where fragments of material may fly around, safety spectacles or a visor must be worn. Where fine dust may be generated a dust mask should also be worn. Of particular danger to the respiratory system are the dusts from sanding machines and electric polishers. Among the most injurious dusts are those from medium-density fibreboard, grindstone grits and polishing mops.

The physical dangers in using sanding machines and polishing motors can be minimized by ensuring that the surface to which you apply your workpiece is either moving away from you or in a downwards direction. You should not hook fingers or thumbs through such things as handles and, if your work is snatched from your hand, let it go rather than risk injury. If your piece of work becomes uncomfortably hot do not hold it in gloves, let it cool before continuing work on it.

You should not use lathes, milling machines nor heavy-duty vertical drills without some formal instruction or the use of the manufacturer's handbook, or a reputable professional engineering manual. Of great importance in the case of vertical drills and milling machines is the use of clamps to hold the work securely.

NOISE

Exposure to excessive industrial noise can damage your hearing and result in a degree of deafness. If you work in a very noisy workshop you should wear some sort of ear protection. A silversmithing workshop in which raising and forging take place or noisy pieces of machinery such as linishers are used is the sort of environment where your hearing is in danger. One of the few activities in which you need to hear what you are doing is planishing; you must hear that clear ringing tone!

CUTTING EQUIPMENT

Cutting equipment that must be used with caution includes guillotines, shears and handsaws. The obvious advice in using guillotines and shears is to think about what you are doing and keep your fingers and thumbs well away from the cutting blades.

In using a bandsaw keep your hands at a distance from the moving blade. You can push the metal towards the blade with a wooden stick; do not force the metal through since a broken blade may fly about. Wear safety spectacles or a visor.

— 5 —

Design

This chapter should be read in conjunction with the illustrations of the design drawings and subsequently finished pieces of work by leading British silversmiths who are members of the Association of British Designer Silversmiths. The illustrations show that no two people work in exactly the same way and this should be of great encouragement to anyone who is beginning life as a designer.

Designing can be a passionate and emotional business and principles are held very dearly indeed, sometimes too much so, and what is admired by one person may be viewed with the utmost contempt by another. These views are usually directed at the perceived intellectual, philosophical or fashion content of a design, not so much at matters such as proportion, detail or even practicability.

For the worker lacking in confidence or the beginner who hopes eventually to make a mark and stand out as a significant and successful designer, this may make life very intimidating. If you are lucky enough to have a teacher or an adviser who looks at your work and talents in an analytical manner, offers sound tutorials and helps you to develop your own individual personality as a designer, then you should have little to worry about for the future.

If you are isolated and wish to develop your design talents then life may be rather more difficult. Naturally if you are learning the craft of making pieces of silver at the same time as making your initial forays into designing, you will be working in a modest way. From a design point of view you will probably be mainly involved in matters of proportion and the variations of one curve or another, probably in relation to simple dishes and bowls. In terms of learning about the metal as you work it, you will develop a feel for it and will discover what happens when you attack it in a particular manner. The reaction of metal to applied stresses and the pleasing forms and movements that result are emphasized in the succeeding chapters on technique. You would, of course, be foolish not to take advantage of any pleasing natural qualities and add them to your design vocabulary.

In studying proportions and in balancing forms one against another there is no standard formula, and if there were the business of design would be extremely limited and dull. You can look to geometrical calculations to solve your problems but these will soon prove of limited use and may end by ruling you and stunting your ability to develop and think for yourself. A much better route to learning about proportion and form is to look around you at everything in your world, from natural forms such as seed pods or sea shells, to man-made forms such as cars, aircraft or bridges and architectural structures. You can also look at the work of leading contemporary designers and, indeed, many people have identified modern heroes in their craft and been inspired thereby. This is quite natural and reasonable, but you must never imitate nor slavishly copy the work of someone else.

Keith Smith: Chased box. The process of chasing has determined the contours, the metal sinking into the pitch to produce natural curves.

Rather use it as a bench mark – a standard for future aspirations.

It is absolutely vital that you should have a system for recording and developing your ideas. The ideal and most economical method is to keep a sketchbook. You may not be, or you may not believe yourself to be, a skilled draftsman, but if you steel yourself to start and keep at it you can only improve. You can also use photography and in some situations it is the only way of recording an image that you see. A macro, or close-up lens may be useful for recording minute structures and textures.

In developing drawings, even if you have not got an expert control over your pencil, you will nevertheless know why you recorded the image and what special features or proportions appealed to you. If in your first drawing you feel that you have not got it quite right, you can overlay it with tracing paper and make the alterations that you feel are necessary and carry on in the same way until you are satisfied.

Some designers use photocopiers and there are high-quality machines which will reduce or enlarge and vary the quality of the development of the image to cope with subtle pencil shadings. This is of particular importance in enlarging thumbnail-sized drawings which otherwise may have to be squared off in order to ensure an accurate enlargement.

You may, however, still be a little unsure

of yourself and, before buying expensive metal, would like to see something a little more realistic than lines on paper. If you are designing, for instance, a dish of a subtle, elongated plan form you might confirm your judgement by cutting a replica of the plan in cardboard. You will have a stand-alone shape which can be further modified if necessary. Any suitable material may be used for models or templates. Thin, medium-density fibreboard is excellent for cutting and sanding accurately. In designing deeper or rounded forms in which planes or curves may intersect and which are difficult to judge on paper, you may make models in wood, card or Plasticine. Model making is a part of the design process and some leading designers make models as a matter of course; an accurate model is also a great help in estimating the amount of metal that is required.

Having now dealt with the possible development of a simple idea, it is important to stress that you should never settle for the first one that comes into your head. You should always develop two or three ideas to quite an advanced stage before selecting the design that you wish to take all the way.

You will not be able to work as a designer for any length of time before you are confronted by the problems of functional requirements, as with a teapot where the spout should pour properly and the handle be well insulated. Knives and forks may demand a consideration of ergonomics, and in the design of many other articles new and significant aspects of designing may become important. It is very easy to allow the technical requirements to dominate you completely and stifle any search for originality, or to make you meekly follow tradition. It must be said, however, that even if you are determined not to be dominated and wish to be in-

novative, while paying due attention to technical requirements, it will not be easy and may be a miserable experience.

Decoration is an area of design that arouses strong emotions and loyalties. There are some designers who have no time for decoration at all and others, but only a few, who are expert and sensitive and who produce fine designs. Talent or inclination apart, decoration is an expensive business in a craft that is work-intensive and involves the use of costly materials, and this is one reason why so little is seen today.

It is possible to suggest two areas for consideration in relation to the decoration of pieces of silver. First of all, what can decoration do for a form or design? Decoration can and should enhance a form so that, for instance, the decoration on a tall, slim form should surely emphasize these characteristics. Alternatively, you may have designed an absolutely sheer, cylindrical container and believe that if the top has the correct scale of decoration, the one will emphasize the quality of the other. The two examples suggest that we come back to a matter of proportions, and also that you can establish your own belief and theory regarding the disposition of decoration.

The second area of consideration concerns the actual form of decoration. You will certainly not be able to develop most ideas other than by drawing. If you are proposing the use of simple geometry and linework you will be involved mainly with proportions, but if you have ambitions to develop complex decorative qualities you will have to search for sources of reference. You may look at natural form and be fascinated by what you discover, and you may settle for an extremely accurate representation of what you have found.

However, if you are producing a realistic

image you must still design it to fit the form to which it is to be applied, in scale and perhaps in movement. You must also consider the material that you are using and the technique that you propose to use. The tools and the technique can be cleverly used in an impressionistic manner to convey the essential qualities of your design and this is far more skilful than slaving to produce a laborious and dead replica of an image. You may find that drawing realistic images begins to pall after a while and you might decide to refine and abstract the essential content, and it is at such a stage that some critics will begin to regard you as a true designer.

Computer-aided design is an area of design activity that is often discussed, but a poll of designer silversmiths reveals that only a few are actively involved in it. It is an area which will undoubtedly develop as more and more people become expert users of computers in the course of their education. Another factor that is inhibiting the use of computers in design is the comparative expense of powerful equipment and the software for three-dimensional design.

A few art and design institutions or university faculties have research and development departments and at least one has short vacation courses that the uninitiated would be well advised to consider. For anyone who is already confident with a computer, an approach to similar departments may elicit information regarding suitable software. One thing should be quite clear, however: those who already use a computer in designing insist that it is a tool; it does not think for you or provide you with wonderful, original ideas.

The work-intensive nature of silversmithing and the associated costs have already been touched upon, and the designing of pieces that reflect your ideas

and philosophy but are put together in a cunning and economical manner is a most difficult business that has to be faced. Apart from the problems of producing your work at a cost that the everyday market can afford, designing to a price often arises in relation to commissions. In working to a commission you should bear in mind that you have almost certainly been approached because the customer likes your work, so do not feel that you must throw overboard all that you believe in. You should establish the value of the commission as soon as you are approached so that you may politely decline if it is totally unrealistic. If it is a tight budget, but possible, then you are confronted with a design challenge which you should relish. This is the moment for you to work out how most easily and quickly to produce a piece with your visual philosophy stamped all over it and at the same time delight your customer. It is the time when design, the visual business, and design, the technical business, become as one, and, if you can rise to the challenge successfully, the satisfaction is immense.

In dealing with commissions you should record in duplicate all the essential and relevant details, such as cost, delivery date and the specification of the proposed work.

When you present your final ideas and design to your customer you must do so in a professional manner so that there is no room left for misunderstandings or confusion. A few scrappy scribbles simply will not do. You should at the very least supply a high-quality drawing, rendered or shaded to convey the shape of the piece. You may even, with a very complex piece, need to provide plans, elevations and sections. The use of differently coloured materials may require a coloured drawing.

A few final notes on design relate to the

future: it is all too easy for you to be fully occupied with your current work and output without giving a thought for the future. The worst scenario is that you are immensely successful, working day and night to satisfy demand, and suddenly it all comes to an end and you realize that your ideas are tired and outdated. Some chance, you may think! However, the point is that you should always be putting aside time for research and development, so that you are reaching into the future.

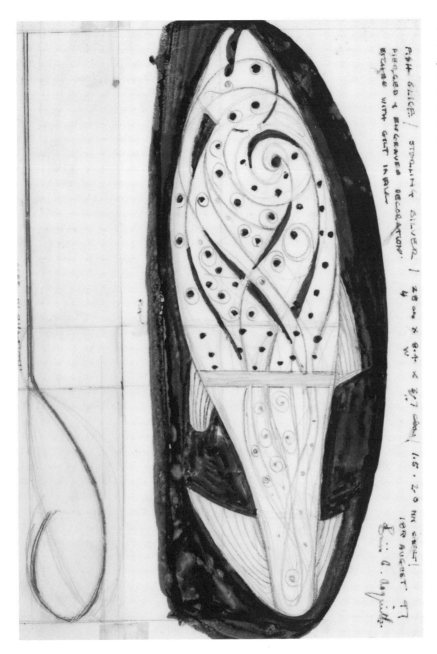

Brian Asquith: Fish slice design. A very good example of stylization and the use of piercing and engraving. Design rendered in pencil and wash.

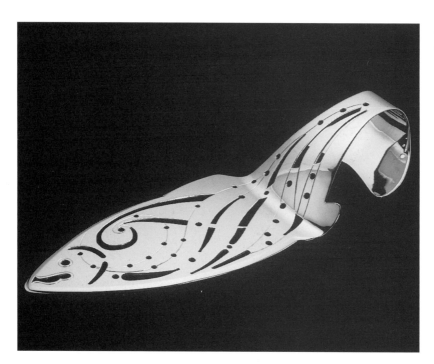

Brian Asquith: Fish slice in silver.

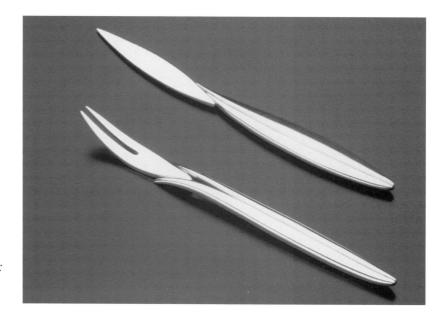

Andrew Bray: Millennium cutlery: Silver salad knife and fork.

Andrew Bray:
Design drawings,
developing ideas.
Pen and ink. First
stage showing the
exploration of several
ideas.

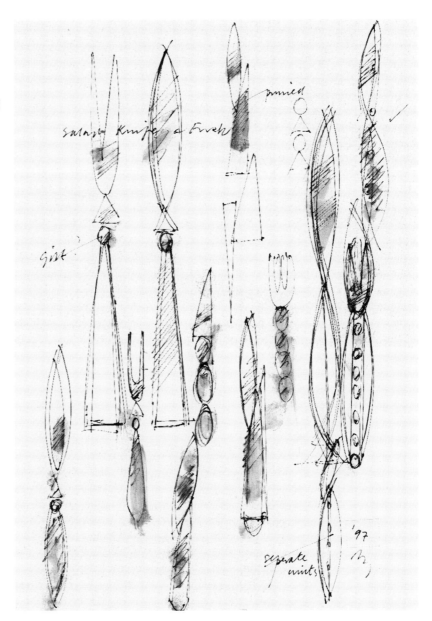

27

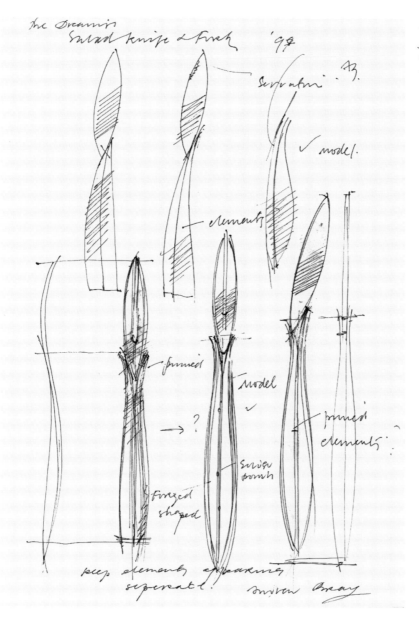

Andrew Bray: the final chosen idea is developed and refined.

*Profile carefully
refined on paper.*

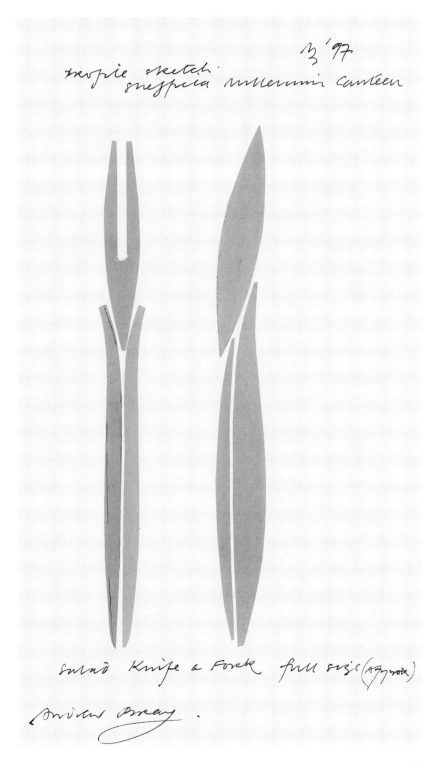

Models in wood.

Andrew Bray: Teapot: Silver and ebony.

Stella Campion: Silver beaker 'Warblers'. Chased and repoussé. Stella uses punches if she can get access to the inside, otherwise she uses a snarling iron. They are then chased and delicately modelled on the outer surfaces.

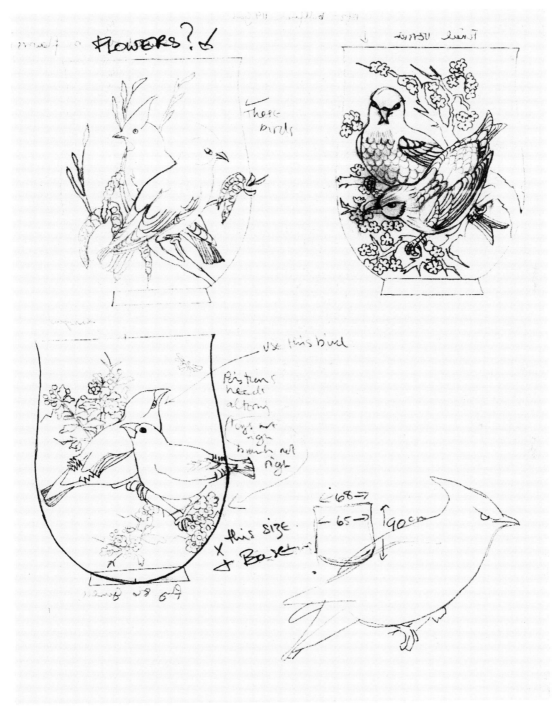

Stella Campion: Original drawings for designs for beaker.

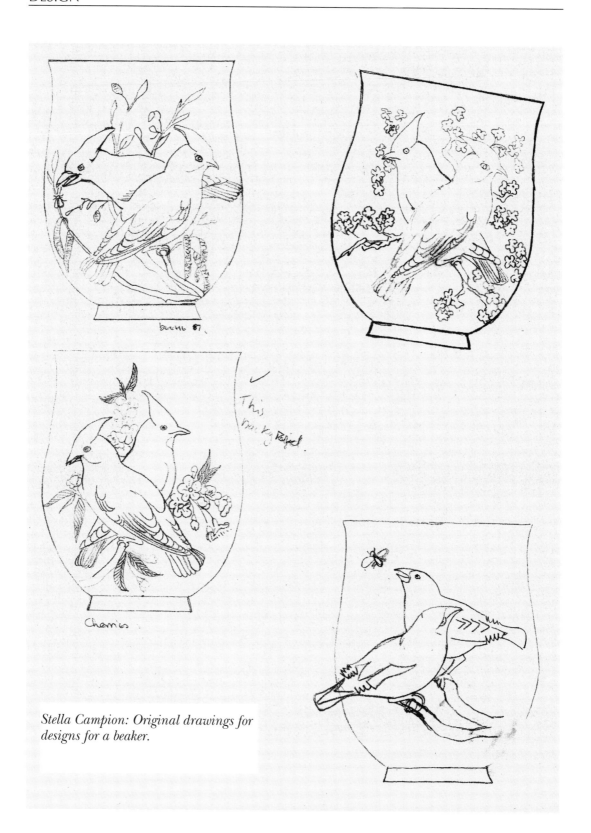

Stella Campion: Original drawings for designs for a beaker.

Howard Fenn: Teapot: Silver and glass.

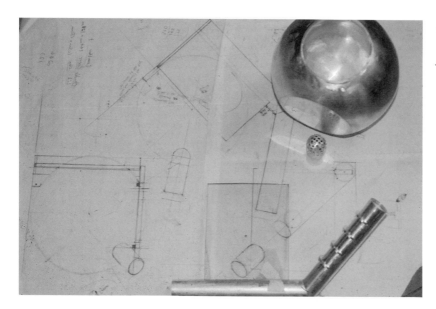

Howard Fenn:
Working design sheet
for teapot.

Wally Gilbert:
Chased vases in
silver.

Wally Gilbert: Design for a slim vase rendered on grey paper in pencil and using white paint to define the highlights and form of the chased decoration. On either side of the central design are shown alternative ideas for decoration. They are shown as developments of the truncated cone to illustrate the decoration all around the vase.

Wally Gilbert: A range of ideas on grey paper using pencil, white paint and yellow paint.

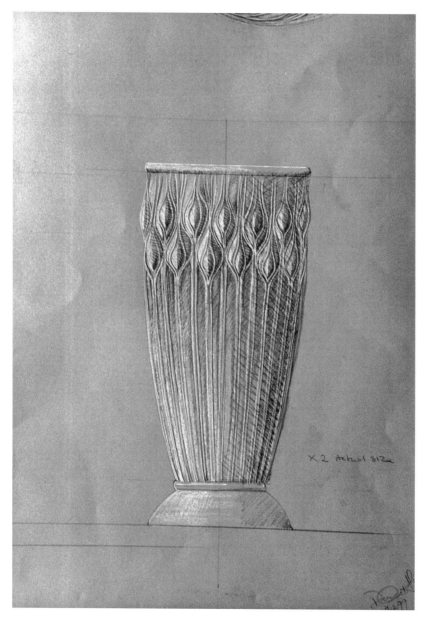

Wally Gilbert: An enlarged illustration of a design for a vase. It clearly shows how pencil shading and white paint can define the form of a design. On this design yellow paint is also used to show applied gold wires.

Kay Ivanovic: Twin-walled 'Pond' beaker, etched and chased silver.

Chris Knight: Pair of candelabra. Worshipful Company of Goldsmiths' Collection.
Silver and gilt with slate bases.

Chris Knight: Spinning teapot with infuser. Silver and polyethylene. Private collection.
This illustration is computer generated using a programme named 'Cinema 4D'.

Chris Knight: 'If you seek me with all your heart' chalice and paten. White metal, gilt, anodized aluminium. St Mary's Church, NYC.

Alistair McCallum: Mokume gane vodka beakers. An extremely important designer with an international reputation for his mokume work.

Alistair McCallum: Design sheet, showing that it is difficult to produce anything more than an impressionistic visual for this technique.

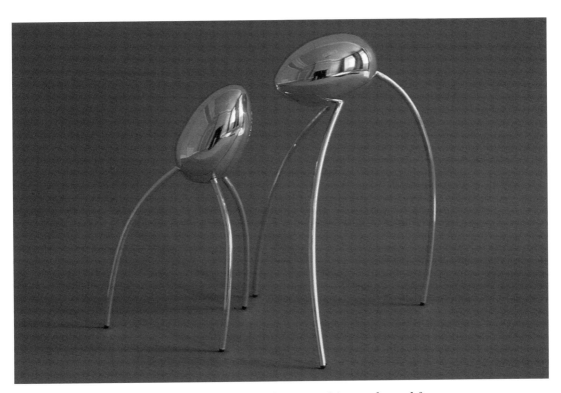

Cara Murphy: Silver condiments tipped with ebony – exciting sculptural forms.

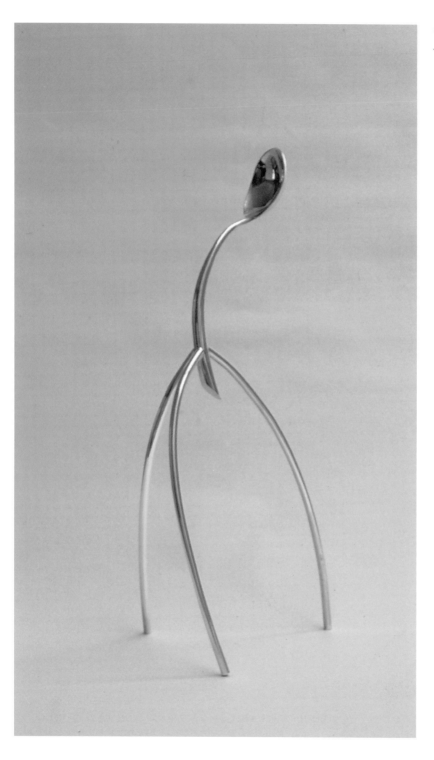

Cara Murphy: Silver spoon.

Cara Murphy: Silver spoons.

*Karin Paynter:
Silver and ceramic
plate, silver cutlery.*

45

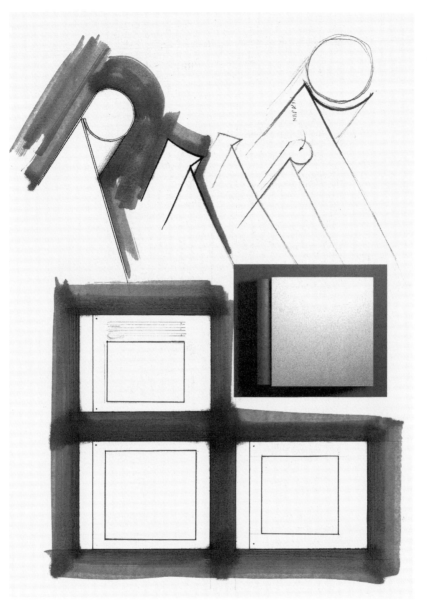

*Karin Paynter:
Silver and ceramic
plate. Early stage
visualizations in
which proportions
and design
variations and
details are
considered. Water-
colour wash is used
to define the
visualizations.*

Karin Paynter: Computer-generated visualization of the basic silver chassis with thoughtful notes. The computer programme '3D Studio Max' was used.

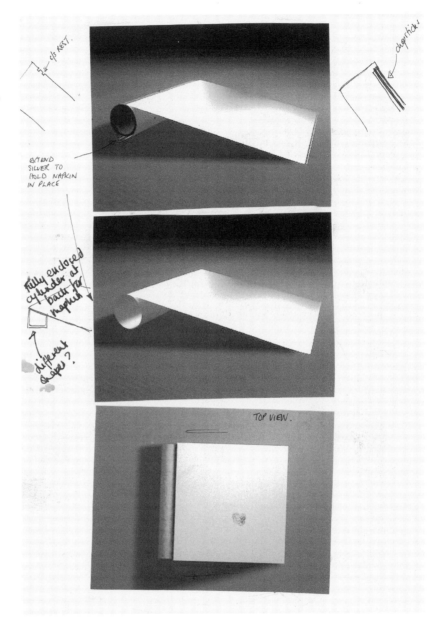

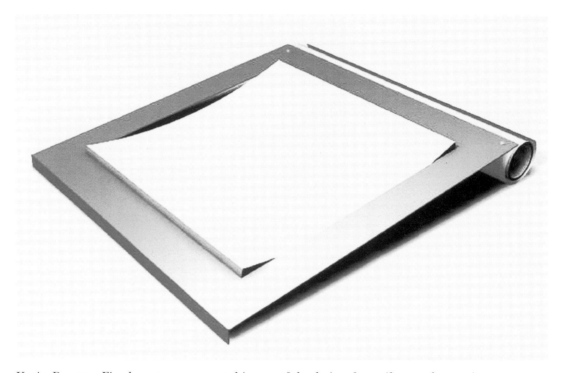

Karin Paynter. Final computer-generated image of the design for a silver and ceramic plate.

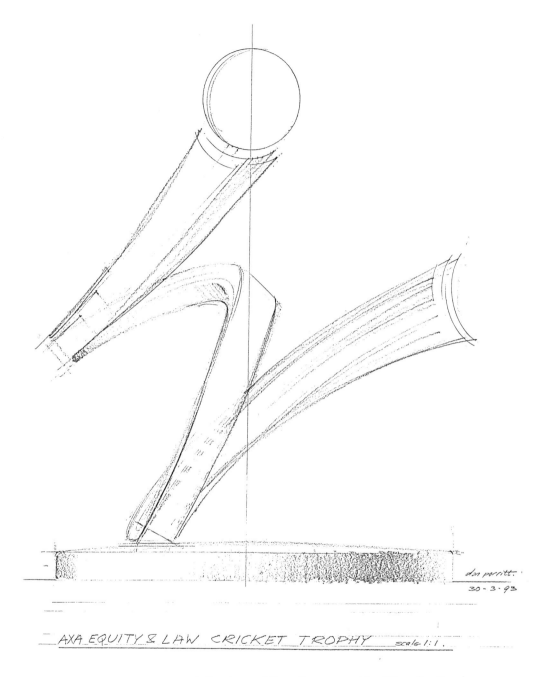

AXA EQUITY & LAW CRICKET TROPHY   scale 1:1.

Don Porrit: Cricketer trophy: AXA Equity and Law League trophy. Visualization in
pencil, the intention of the designer is clearly to symbolize the trajectory of a cricket ball.
An advanced design presentation using white crayon on black paper is shown on page
50 together with a photograph of the finished piece.

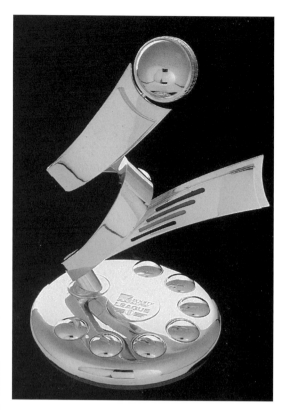

Don Porrit: AXA cricket trophy:
Silver plated and enamelled.
Design and finished piece shown.

Don Porrit: Silver wine flagon – a very fine sculptural form.

Martyn Pugh: Orbital tea pot: silver and recycled ebony.

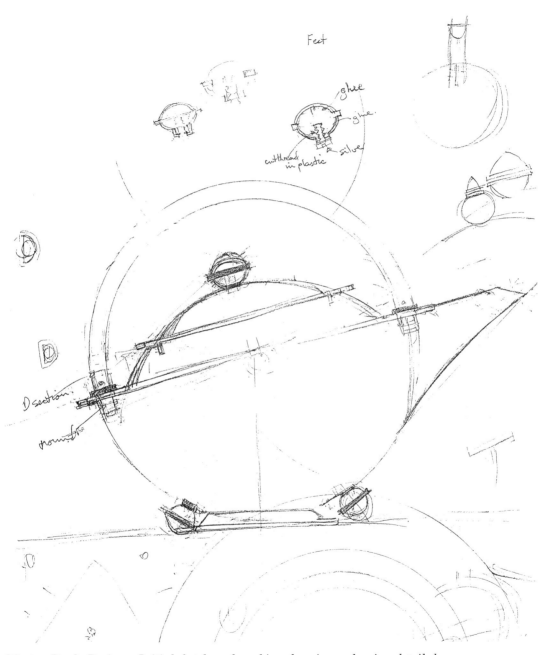

Feet

ghee

glue

cut thread
in plastic

silver

D section

nourish

Martyn Pugh: Designs: Initial sketch and working drawings, showing detailed construction being worked out. These sketches would be supplemented by construction notes and calculations.

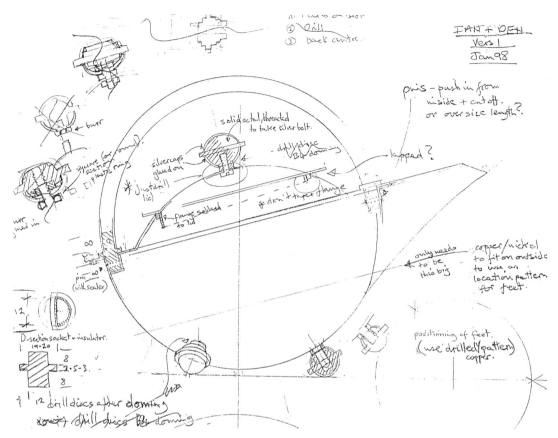

Martyn Pugh. This illustration shows exactly the careful planning that is needed before a design can be made up. Apparently simple components such as the knob and the feet are clever little structures that must be considered carefully in terms of technical construction as well as in aesthetic detailing. The drawing of the sections of the lid and body joint allow the exact dimensions of flanges, thickening wires and the bezel to be determined. Such diagrams and the thought in producing them can also help to determine a logical order in which components may be soldered together. In this design considerable thought was given to producing an insulated handle which fitted into the body without the use of large external sockets. The section shows internal body sockets and proposed methods of pinning the handle.

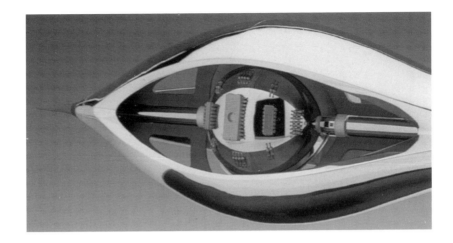

Martyn Pugh: University of Hertfordshire mace, showing superb symbolism of the scientific and engineering base of the institution.

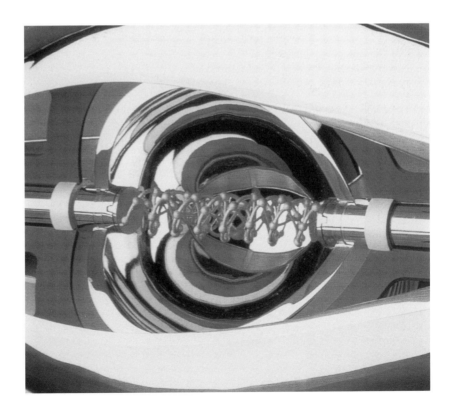

Keith Smith: Full-size wooden mock-up, to determine exact form and to help estimate the amount of metal required.

Keith Smith: Two-cup silver teapot with ebony handle and thumb-piece. Photograph by Keith Thompson.

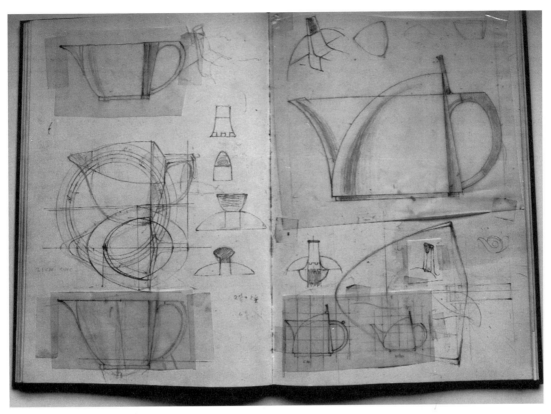

Keith Smith: Print of sketchbook pages on which the design was developed from a thumbnail drawing which was squared off and then enlarged to full-size. Tracing paper was then placed over the enlargement and alterations made. All drawings in pencil.

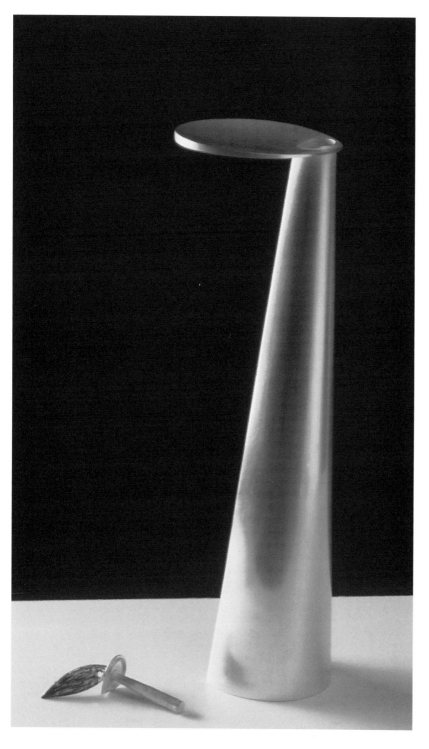

Simone Ten Hompel: Silver carafe, height 48cm. The designer does not belong to the 'Mirror Polish School' but is an expert in producing unique, sensitive and finely textured surfaces.

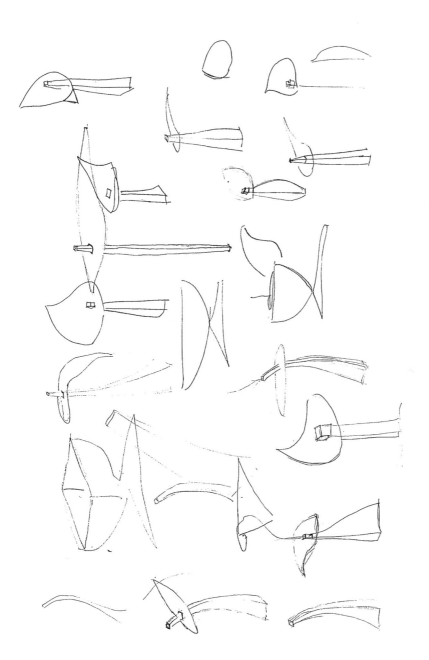

Simone Ten Hompel: Design work for the carafe drawn directly in pen and ink.

59

Simone Ten Hompel. Preliminary thoughts on the form of the carafe.

— 6 —

Sinking

Sinking is the simplest of all the forming techniques and is used to produce dishes and bowls of a variety of depths and for varying uses. Straightforward dishes and bowls form one category of product and others might include ladle bowls and chalice bowls. Any shape of vessel can be produced, from circular to oval, and triangular to quartic.

The first need in producing any object is to determine the size of the piece of metal that is required. This piece is always known as the blank. Determining the size of the blank for a sinking is as simple as the technique itself. You simply cut a piece of metal that is identical to the plan form of your design, both in size and shape.

The thickness of metal that you will use must also be determined. For small and comparatively shallow forms a metal thickness of 1.1mm is adequate, although for larger shallow forms 1.3mm will display a stronger looking edge. The thickness of 1.5mm will be adequate for vessels of medium depth, although for a luxurious and strong look 1.8mm will be very good. All of these thicknesses are standard gauges that are available at all metal dealers.

Having decided upon your metal thickness you must cut it to the required shape. For the gauges up to 1.5mm you will be able to use a pair of shears, but thicker metal will have to be cut with a saw unless you have a guillotine. If you find cutting metal with shears to be hard work, put one handle in the bench vice and bear down on the other with your hand, backed up if necessary with shoulder pressure. After cutting the blank, trim any inaccuracies with a file and remove any sharp burrs.

Before the metal is worked it must be softened by heating it with a large, hot flame, revolving the hearth to ensure an even heating, until the metal becomes a dull red. The heat should be maintained for a few moments to ensure a complete softening. This process is known as annealing. The blank may then be either allowed to cool or, alternatively, grasped in tongs and plunged while hot into cold water in a sink or a large bucket. When some non-ferrous metals such as silver and gilding metal are quenched in cold water they may become up to 25 per cent softer than if they are allowed to cool naturally in air. The author always quenches silver when sinking and raising but does not quench flat sheet or boxes because of the possibility that distortion may occur. After quenching, the metal should be placed in pickle to clean off surface oxides. When silver has been annealed and pickled it emerges white in colour with a matt surface, which is a real advantage because then marks from a polished hammer show up as polished metal, so indicating how accurately the hammering is proceeding. Copper and gilding metal display similar characteristics: matt and pinkish after pickling and bright when hammered.

Before hammering begins, concentric pencil lines 1cm apart should be scribed upon the surface of the blank. If the blank is circular use a pair of compasses fitted with a pencil; but any other shape will require you to work around the edge of the blank, holding the pencil between your thumb and first two fingers, and using your third finger to regulate the distance between the lines. The scribed lines must be renewed each time that the blank is worked so that the shape of the vessel is kept accurate and true.

To form the vessel, the blank is hammered on a steel plate, which should be clean, unmarked and polished if possible. If the plate is very heavy it may rest on the bench, but if it is light and likely to move then it should be held in the vice. A hammer with a domed face is used, a gentle, curved dome at first, and for shallow dishes, and a well-rounded dome for deeper forms. For very shallow dishes in thin metal a wooden mallet with a pear-shaped head may be used.

The hammering of the metal begins on the outer scribed line which is 1cm inside the edge of the blank. The blank is rotated as it is hammered on the steel block and each hammer blow should overlap its neighbour. When the first row of hammering is completed then another row is started, overlapping the first, and this action continues row upon row until the centre of the blank is reached. If you work as accurately as suggested, not only will your vessel be true in form but you will also exact the maximum effect from each

Marking out.

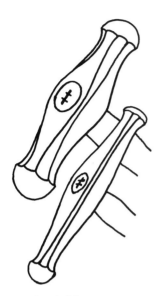

Hammers for sinking.

course of work and save time and effort in the long run.

The action that has been described thins the metal and causes an expansion of the surface; but because the outer rim of the blank has not been hammered, and therefore the diameter of the blank has not been increased, a dish is formed.

When sinking oval and elongated shapes or square shapes, each row of hammering should be alternated in direction, clockwise and anti-clockwise, otherwise a severe twisting of the form will take place as the metal moves in one direction.

After the whole surface of the metal has been hammered, the grain structure of the metal has become distorted and work-hardened. Before more work is carried out

Sinking.

Sinking. A section to show the hammering action.

the metal must annealed and annealed again after any subsequent work. To work metal for too long without annealing will result in disastrous cracking of the surface and its eventual disintegration.

As courses of sinking proceed, the dish or bowl will become deeper and you must obviously keep an eye on the shape, checking the profile against your design elevation, or use a cardboard template. Any unevenness of the edge profile can easily be corrected with hand pressure, using the palms to squeeze inwards or the thumbs to force outwards. You can also press the edge of the form against the bench.

A circular dish will not usually distort to any great degree so long as it is held at a constant angle as it is revolved and hammered. However. in the case of oval and elongated shapes the ends will tend to rise as work proceeds and, as a result, a rather attractive curved profile will complement the form of the vessel. This is a practical lesson in design, something to be noted and remembered. It may be a good idea, within reason, to go where the metal leads you and to take advantage of what happens when particular stresses are applied through working techniques. You must naturally retain ultimate control over the aesthetics and any practical purpose that the piece may have must be respected.

As already suggested, you can modify the

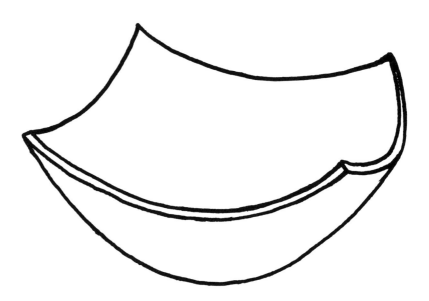

Sinking a square blank.

shape of an elongated form by pressing the sides against the bench, so narrowing the vessel and lowering the ends. This should be done while the metal is hard so that it will move evenly. Alternatively, you can widen the vessel, resting it on a sandbag and pushing on the inside edges, making it more shallow and raising the ends.

You can ensure a positive and prominent variation of the profile of a dish or bowl by marking out a square blank with circular, scribed lines and working to these lines.

The corners of the square will rise in a prominent manner. As already stated, you will have to work each row of hammering in an alternating direction in order to avoid a twisting and distortion of the square form.

As you near the end of a sinking operation you should work at least one course of hammering with light blows, so that when planishing begins there will be no excessively deep marks to remove. The technique of planishing is described in Chapter 9.

Raising

Raising is a technique that is used to produce vessels that are deep or of medium depth from one sheet of metal, usually a disc. There are two distinct methods of working: the first to be described involves raising the metal from near the centre of the disc, and the second involves a gradual working back towards the centre. The author was taught to work by the first method but many people use the second, or even a combination of the two.

The action is quite different from sinking, where thick metal is stretched to achieve depth. In raising the blank is calculated in a more complex manner and is always much larger than the plan form of the design, and hammering reduces it in diameter to gain height. The metal that is used is also, at 0.9mm thick, much thinner than that used in sinking.

To establish the precise size of the blank that is required to raise a specific form you will need a full-size side elevation of your design and from this you will take the necessary measurements. If you have made a full-size model of your design then you may measure that.

For a form in which the major part of the surface is to be hammered, such as a beaker, a well-rounded shape or a tall, coffee-pot type of form, you should measure the height and estimate the average diameter, as shown in the diagram. The sum of these two measurements represents the diameter of the blank that you will need to produce your designed form.

In the case of a vessel with a wide base

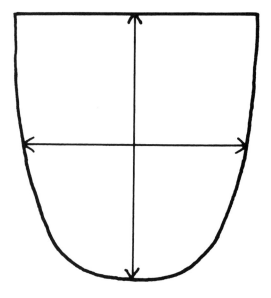

Raising – blank estimate. Average diameter and height.

and of no great height you should add together the measurements of the height and the full width to arrive at the diameter of the blank.

It must be emphasized that individual craftsmen hammer in different ways; some tend to thin the metal and stretch it while others may thicken it. The former practice makes the vessel too large and the latter makes it too small. Experience helps you to make allowance for your technique, although it must be said that if you thin your metal excessively you will simply have to improve your technique.

As we have already indicated, the most

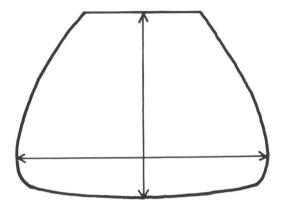

Raising – estimating height and diameter.

common gauge of metal that is used for raising is 0.9mm, although you may use 0.7mm, and for luxurious, heavy pieces you may use 1.1mm. These are standard thicknesses of metal that should be obtainable from your metal dealer, and, if you require a circular blank in silver, the dealer should be able to supply one of any diameter that you specify.

Before raising begins, and whichever method you use, the metal is hollowed on a leather sandbag using a wooden mallet that has a pear-shaped head. The blank should be scribed with concentric pencil circles, and hammering should begin from the centre of the blank, working outwards

Raising – hollowing.

in circles towards the edge. The extreme edge will become crinkled and wavy and should be smoothed with mallet blows on to a wood surface; this spares the surface of the leather sandbag from being lacerated by the sharp edge of the metal.

Hollowing may also be carried out by malleting the metal into a shallow hollow in a block of wood. In some workshops a length of tree trunk stands on the floor with several hollows cut into the top surface and with a variety of useful grooves and channels around the edge. Hollowing produces a shallow dish and it may be carried out more than once, but the metal must not be thinned as in sinking. It must be annealed after each course of work.

When hollowing has been completed, raising may begin But first the tools that are to be used must be described and illustrated. The steel tools upon which the raising and hammering takes place are called stakes. In point of fact, this is an all-embracing name that is applied to any steel form on which silver and other metals are hammered. Custom-made raising stakes may be purchased but may prove to be too expensive for those who are just estab-lishing a workshop. A perfectly satisfactory stake can easily be made from a short length of round steel bar, which will be held in a vice during use. Suitable bars might be found in a scrapyard or as stub ends in an engineering works. The author does most of his raising on a round bar that is 280mm (11in) long and 50mm (2in) in diameter. On the end that is used for raising, the face of the bar is cut away at an angle and the edge is rounded, as shown in the diagram. A gentle curve runs back along the top surface of the bar for about 30mm (1¼in). For raising smaller objects smaller bars may be used, but you should always use the largest one possible for the job in hand. To use one which is too light will result in a loss of the full effect of each hammer blow because the stake will 'give' a little. The inside of the vessel will also be deeply marked as the narrow curve bites into the surface. In raising many designs stakes which are more rounded may be needed. Once again there is a range of stakes that may be purchased and which will fulfil most needs. You may also be able to modify bars and, if there is a blacksmith in your area, have something bent to your specification.

It is vital that if you saw or file steel in your workshop, where you also work silver, you must carefully collect all silver filings before you start working the steel, and that you are equally careful in collecting all steel filings when you have finished working the steel. You must never get silver

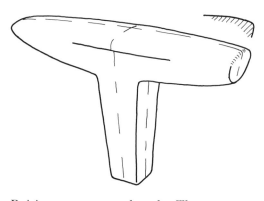

Raising – custom-made stake. The stem can fit into a hole in a low bench. Raising to be done as the craftsman sits.

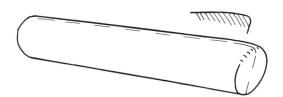

Raising bar modified in the workshop.

scrap tainted with ferrous metal filings because your bullion dealer will be extremely unhappy if you send such a mixture for smelting and reclamation.

The actual raising of metal is carried out with a raising hammer which is a specialist tool and may only be purchased as such. The head of the hammer has one narrow, flat face which is used for the raising, and one narrow, curved face that can be used for forging and stretching metal. When purchased the flat surface of the hammer will have sharp edges and these must be softened, as illustrated. Sharp edges, if not removed, will cut and damage the surface of the vessel that is being raised. The standard raising hammer, as purchased, is suitable for most projects and certainly for anything as large as you will wish to raise. For small forms you may need a lighter

hammer with a narrower face. You could in this instance modify a standard hammer. You may need to use a grindstone, and if so you must use a visor or safety spectacles. It is most important that both stakes and hammers have clean and polished working surfaces so that no damaging marks are hammered into the surface of the vessel that is being made. Polishing hammers and stakes are dealt with in Chapter 14 on finishing and polishing.

Raising may also be carried out using a modified tinman's mallet. The mallet must have a hardwood head and one face is cut to a wedge shape, as illustrated. The wedge face is used for the actual raising and will wear quite quickly and thus will need resharpening. Some craftsmen prefer to use a mallet in the very early stages of raising, and it can also be of great help in later stages if you have thinned the metal excessively. The softer blows of the mallet allow the metal to thicken up.

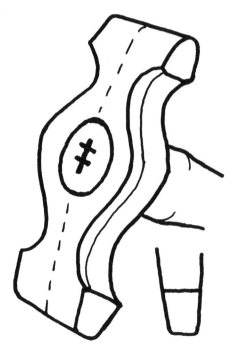

Raising hammer.

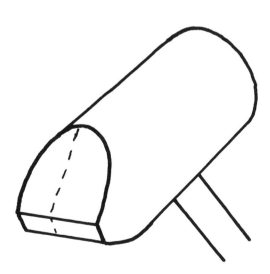

Mallet for raising.

RAISING: METHOD 1

The tools and equipment having been described, the technique of raising may now be explained. First you need to know at which point on your sunken-dish form you should start the raising. Sight the profile of your dish over your design drawing and establish at what point the forms differ. Mark this point on the outside, concave surface of the dish and from this point scribe concentric circles right up to the outer edge by using a pencil and a pair of compasses.

It is most important that accurate concentric pencil lines are scribed on the vessel before each raising because it is on an adherence to these lines that the symmetry of the form depends. To scribe the lines on a deep form may prove a problem because it becomes difficult to work from the centre with ordinary compasses, which will become too short to reach down the side. Basic compasses are expendable and so their arms may be bent, or two pairs may be lashed or soldered together to make one pair with a 'double elbow'.

You should now place the dish with its

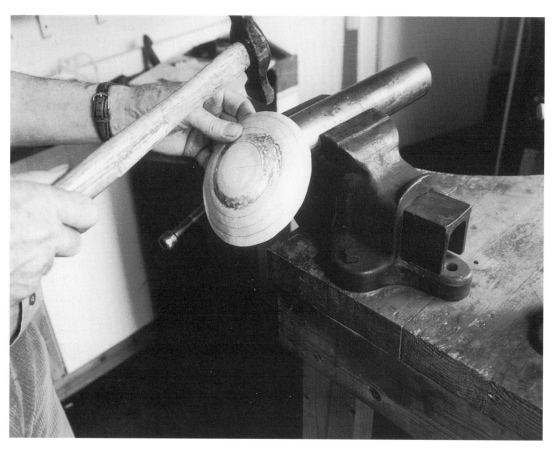

Raising.

inside surface in contact with the rounded nose of the raising stake at the point at which you wish to commence raising. The outer edge of the dish must be raised above the surface of the stake, leaving space between the stake and the inside of the dish. If you now strike the dish surface with your raising hammer, very close to the point of contact, its surface will be driven down on to the stake. If you continue hammering, turning the metal and following the scribed line, a step will be formed all around it, as shown in the diagram. You should now start another row of hammering, still keeping the edge of the dish above the stake surface, and then follow with new

courses, moving the step all the while up the dish and so narrowing it in diameter.

You should not attempt to raise too much metal at a time. To reduce the diameter of the work by 12mm (fiin) in each raising is quite sufficient, and if you are raising a tall, narrow form you may have to settle for less. To attempt to reduce the diameter of your vessel by a great amount may be disastrous, resulting in the metal being folded over on to itself and necessitating soldered joints which will always show up and may break during subsequent raising. If you do find yourself in this plight you can attempt to save the day only by carefully nursing the metal down on to the stake with a wooden mallet.

As your raising advances up the side of the vessel, you should move it back towards you so that you are always hammering close to the nose of the stake, as illustrated. This prevents the metal from bucking, bouncing and hurting the hand that holds it. Your hammering must be consistent and even, slightly overlapping each hammer mark and each row of hammer marks, otherwise the body will become inaccurate in form, and the top edge will become uneven.

When you have raised the vessel to within 6mm (⁄in) of the top edge you should take a wooden or horn mallet and drive down what will be a crinkled edge on to the surface of the raising stake. This will prevent damage to the raising stake from an inaccurate hammer blow or any thinning action on the edge of the vessel.

The final action in a course of raising is to thicken the edge of the vessel, a process known as caulking. Before the vessel is annealed it should be positioned on a sandbag and you should hold it in place with a hand spread across the mouth while you hammer directly down on to the edge with the raising hammer, as illustrated.

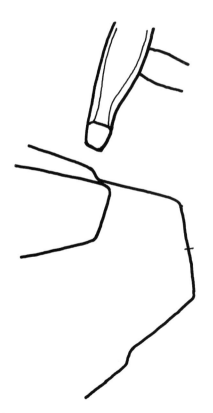

Raising.

The vessel should be rotated and hammered all round its circumference. This process is carried out after every raising, and by the time a piece is fully raised its edge may be doubled into a thickness that tapers down into the body.

After each raising the metal will be extremely hard and must be annealed before any more work is carried out. You must make sure that you anneal silver carefully and ensure that it is properly softened. Place your work on the hearth face down and turn the hearth as you apply heat. Silver that has not been properly softened may begin to crack in the later stages of a raising, and equally silver that

Raising equipment.

Raising – caulking.

has been overheated may also begin to fall apart as a result of the enlargement of its grain structure.

As the raising of a vessel continues you should regularly check the profile of the developing form against your drawing so that you know when the required shapes and diameters have been achieved. As one part of the form is completed you will need to start your raising higher up the body. When the vessel is close to the required shape you can both use visual judgement and measurements to decide when you have achieved your objective or you may make a cardboard template that can be fitted to the form.

Your final course of raising should be undertaken with great care, hammering very accurately so as not to leave any deep cuts or gashes on the surface of the metal because this makes the process of

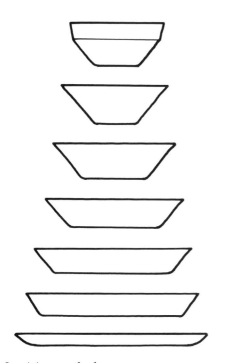

No. 2 raising method.

planishing much easier and takes less time.

If the edge of the mouth of the vessel is uneven after raising it may be trimmed to a scribed line with a file. If it is extremely uneven, or the vessel is too high, the surplus metal may be removed by using shears. You should scribe a guide line and, holding the vessel with the mouth facing your body, you should use the shears to cut in an anti-clockwise direction. If you try to cut in a clockwise direction the shears will cut diagonally into the body.

RAISING: METHOD 2

In the method to be described the importance of the use of scribed lines, of the hammer and of the position of the metal on the stake are exactly the same as already described.

First a line should be scribed on the outside surface of the sunken form about 2.5cm (1in) from the outer edge. The metal should be raised from this point and the final edge should be malleted on to the stake. After annealing and pickling, a new line should be scribed about 6mm (¼in) closer to the centre of the vessel, and another complete course of raising to the outer edge undertaken. This procedure should be repeated until you have worked back to the vicinity of the base of your design. Once this stage has been reached then you go back to the original starting point 2.5cm from the edge and repeat what has already been described. The diagrams illustrate the stages in the procedure. You should caulk the edge of the vessel after each raising and be alert as to the shape of your raised form in relation to the profile and dimensions of your designs so that you know at what stage you should stop raising.

It remains only to describe one or two variations in raising. The first relates to

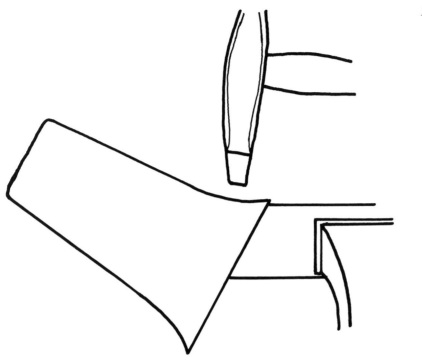

Raising – flare.

flared forms, either trumpet or tulip-shaped. You can raise the vessel to the required diameter as a conical form, as illustrated. You should then point your raising stake away from you and, with the mouth of the vessel facing you, begin to raise down the form, gradually raising less metal as you go. In this way you establish a flare to the vessel. It may be that the flare becomes too deep for the hammer to reach in from one end, in which case you may be able to work from both ends of the vessel.

The final technique involves thickening the bottom of a raised form to make it strong for a base. It may also be used if you have made your vessel a little too tall. First scribe circles from the point at which you wish to raise, usually at the base line. You now need a stake which will fit into the body and have a curve similar to that which is required. Placing the vessel over the stake, you begin to hammer on the outer line and raise the metal working in towards the centre. Close to the centre a pimple will be formed and it will need some force to drive it down on to the stake. It is also possible to achieve something close to what has been described by working 'on air', that is, resting your vessel face down on the bench and hammering with a flatfaced hammer or mallet in circles from the centre outwards.

Planishing your vessel to finish is the subject of Chapter 9.

— 8 —

Seaming

In this chapter the term seaming refers to the production of hollow objects that are made by shaping a sheet of metal around a steel bar or tapered mandrel and soldering the seam that is formed where the edges of the metal meet.

It is a technique that has been much used in the past in the production of almost any vessel that may be imagined. The author has been involved in the restoration of many pieces of eighteenth- and nineteenth-century pieces of silver, including two-handled cups, sugar casters, teapots and coffee pots, mainly with curvilinear profiles, and, with only a few exceptions, they have all been seamed. Several with complex profiles were made up of more than one seamed form, one soldered on top of another, normally with a wire between them to give an architectural emphasis and to conceal the joint.

I discovered therefore that raising, which many consider to be the ultimate forming skill, was hardly ever used during the time that might be considered the golden period of British silversmithing.

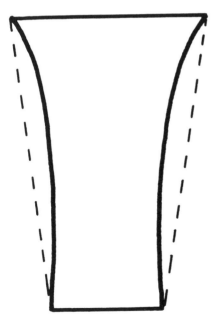 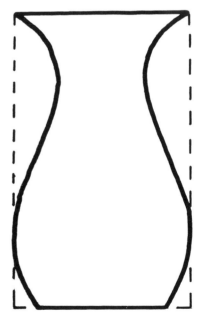

Seaming – calculating blanks, curvilinear forms. The broken lines on the diagrams indicate forms from which the curved designs will be made; a truncated cone for the trumpet shape and a cylinder for the duo-curved shape.

One might surmise that this state of affairs demonstrates, as ever, that making a living comes first and that so long as a design can be produced superbly, the fastest method of production must be used. It must, however, be emphasized that the technique, although fast in producing a result, is not just an easy way out. A high standard of craftsmanship is required.

To calculate the blank of metal for a seamed body you must have a full-scale drawing of the side elevation of your design. There are only two relevant calculations and they are for a cylinder or for a truncated cone. If your design is straight-sided, cylindrical or conical, its shape will emerge as soon as the metal blank is worked around a steel bar or mandrel. However, if your design has a curvilinear form you will have to decide from which of the two basic forms, cylindrical or conical, that it can the more easily be produced. It is a simple and logical decision, as the diagrams show. After the basic forming on a bar or mandrel the curvilinear form is attained by raising.

The calculations involved in producing a blank of metal for a cylinder are extremely simple. You measure the height of the cylinder for one dimension and multiply the diameter by 3.14 to arrive at the other dimension, hence a cylinder 150mm high x 50mm in diameter would need a blank of metal 150mm x 157mm.

In the case of a truncated cone the precise elevation must be drawn on a large piece of paper. The side lines of the elevation are extended to intersect and complete the cone and this intersection becomes the centre from which pencil compasses are used to scribe arcs through both the narrow and the wide end of the elevation. With a pair of dividers, measure the diameter of the base of the cone and mark this distance on the arc on either side of the base, adding on one side a distance equal to one-seventh of the base diameter. Now join these points to the point of the cone. The blank that is required is that area that is defined on the one hand by the two pencilled arcs and on the other by the outer side lines.

The usual gauge of metal that is used for a seamed design is 0.9mm. Obviously a thicker gauge may be used, but unless the design is very small, thinner gauges should be used with caution because any inaccuracy in the joint may result in a very thin area after cleaning up.

If you are using silver take careful overall measurements of your estimated blank and order the smallest possible rectangle or square of metal. If you need similar metal for other parts of your design it may be worth cutting paper or card templates of each component and arranging them together so as to be able to order one sheet to be used economically with as little scrap left over as possible.

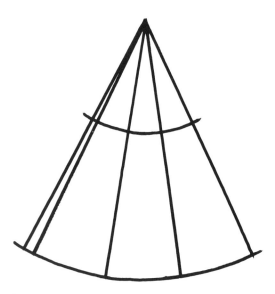

Seaming – truncated cone.

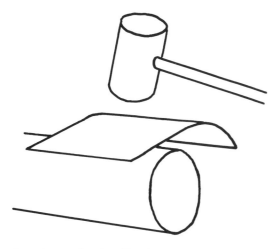

Seaming – shaping blank.

The pattern of the blank should be marked out on the metal by using a metal scriber, with the aid of a metal ruler, a tri-square or a pair of dividers, as appropriate. In cutting the metal to shape the most fortunate craftsman may have the use of a treadle or long-handled bench guillotine, but many will possess only metalworker's shears. The easiest way to use the shears is to fasten one handle in the vice and to press down on the other with one hand, while feeding the metal into the shears with the other hand. Make sure that you keep your fingers and thumb well clear of the cutting blades of the shears. After cutting, the edges of the metal blank may be rippled and distorted, but you may

Seaming first stage – shaping each end over a bar with a boxwood Tinmans mallet.

remedy this by using a Tinmans mallet to straighten them out on a metal plate or a flat, wooden surface. Convex curved lines can be cut with shears, but concave curves may be better cut with a piercing saw.

After cutting the blank you should trim it with a file, making sure that it is accurate in every way and that all sharp burrs are removed. You should then anneal and pickle it, ready for forming on a steel bar or tapered mandrel. The metal will be worked around the bar or mandrel with a Tinmans mallet, which must have a clean, smooth surface because a rough and broken wood grain may make deep, damaging, marks on the surface of a soft metal. The bar or mandrel upon which you

form the metal should be a little smaller in diameter than the intended diameter of the finished piece. For instance, an 80mm (3in)-diameter cylinder might be formed over a 65mm (2fiin)-diameter bar.

To shape your blank of metal you first curve one edge over the bar or mandrel, using the mallet and, working from one end to the other, as illustrated. You may work a second row of mallet blows, but you do not work right across the blank. Instead you turn it round and work the other edge around the bar. These curves should be very close to the curvature required on the finished piece. At this stage of the operation you have a blank with two curved edges and a flat area between them. To

Continuing the curving of the blank by hand.

Seaming springing joint.

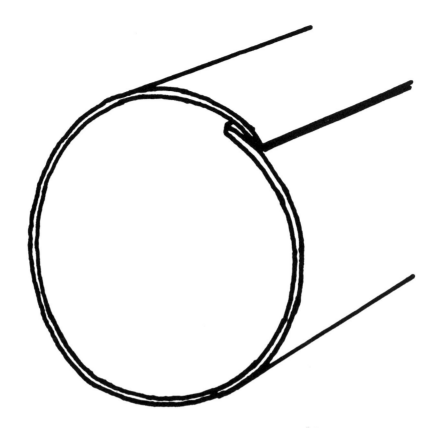

bend the rest of the blank and to bring the edges together you should place it on the bar or mandrel and bend it using pressure from your hands, spread across the surface to exert an even pressure. It is better to work from one curved side towards the centre of the blank at first and then to work similarly from the other side, gradually working to the centre until the edges meet. The edges will not make a tight, close joint at this stage, but if you can push one edge under and past the other and then let go, the metal will spring outwards and, with the right degree of pressure, will make a good joint.

At this stage you may find that there is only a tight contact between the edges of the blank at the centre of the joint and that

each end is open to a small extent. Filing and malleting will correct this. It is important that the joint is aligned in every way because you cannot fill gaps with solder and edges which do not line up and leave a step on the surface will require excessive filing after soldering, leaving thin and weak areas of metal. When you have finally fitted the joint you should anneal the piece of work and pickle it. Do not quench it, the shock may distort the joint. After pickling the joint should be cleaned with a file or abrasive paper so that the surfaces are bright, shiny and oxide-free.

At this stage the process of soldering must be considered. If you are working in silver you must use assayable solder, available from your bullion dealer; but it is also true that the same solders are used with gilding metal and copper. Solders for use with silver are the enamelling, hard, medium, easy and extra-easy grades. There is one grade, easy-flo, which must never be used with silver because it is not pure enough for hallmarking standards.

It makes sense when soldering a seam to use a solder with the highest melting point, because this leaves a range of solders with lower melting points for all the other joints. The silver solder with the highest melting point is enamelling solder and, although care and concentration is required when it is used on silver, it is the ideal one for a seam because it is difficult to remelt during subsequent solderings and its colour is close to that of silver itself.

A vital stage in soldering is the maintaining of a clean joint during heating because solder will not run and join dirty surfaces. To do this the joint must be painted with a borax solution before any heat is applied. Borax as used by silversmiths may be purchased as a hard, white cone that is ground with water in a shallow, coarse surfaced dish to produce a creamy paste. Borax cones and the dish may be purchased at a silversmith's tool shop. You can also buy powdered borax at a chemist's shop, but this form will be very pure and tends to boil and froth excessively when it is heated. After grinding, the borax paste is painted on to the seam, inside and outside. Paint the borax neatly, the more you spread it across the surface, the further the solder will spread and the more tedious the cleaning up will be, especially inside the body.

The body must now be secured in such a way that the joint will not spring apart during the heating and soldering. This is accomplished by the use of iron binding wire. The wire can be bought at a silversmith's tool shop in loose coils or on plastic bobbins. The most useful thickness is 0.71mm, while for small, delicate pieces 0.56mm is suitable. You can also buy similar wire at an ironmonger's or some florists' shops, but on no account should you use wire with a bright or silvery colour because it may be zinc- or tin-plated, which will damage your silver.

To bind a cylinder is extremely simple. You require several lengths of binding wire with loops twisted at their midpoints. The wire is simply wrapped around the cylinder and the ends are twisted together over the seam. You will need four or five wires, equally spaced, to bind the average

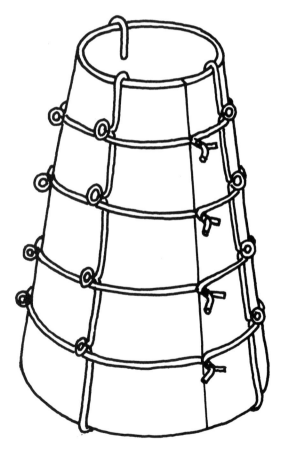

Wired cone seaming.

cylinder and to tighten the wires you should simply twist the back loops and the ends over the seam. Do not tighten the wires excessively, otherwise they will bite into the surface of the metal during heating. When the ends of the wires are twisted together over the joints, tiny, triangular spaces are left which allow the solder to flow under the wires and not solder it to the body.

Wiring a truncated cone is a little more complicated because a wire placed around a tapered form will simply slip off when it is tightened. To overcome this problem you should cut three lengths of wire which are appreciably longer than the length of the cone. On each length four or five loops should be twisted at equal distances apart.

Two of the wires are placed on the body on either side of the seam and their projecting ends should be bent over the top and the bottom edge. The third wire is secured in a similar manner, but on the body directly opposite the seam. Wires similar to those described for the cylinder can now be wrapped around the body, but passing through the loops of the longitudinal wires or on the wide side of them, so that when they are tightened they cannot slip off the cone. After wiring either a cylinder or a cone the joint should be inspected and, if necessary, the borax renewed. The wired cone is illustrated.

It is now time to consider the process of soldering, and the methods that are to be described are those that are used in almost

Seaming soldering.

every situation in silversmithing. There are two basic methods: the first is where the solder, in the form of a strip or stick, is held in a pair of tongs and applied to the joint when it has been heated to the requisite temperature. To reach this stage with a seamed body, and indeed any other object, you should heat it with a large flame passed continuously back and forth while you rotate the hearth. When the metal becomes red hot concentrate the heat for a few moments on the back of the body and then swing round to the joint. Make sure that both sides of the seam are equally hot and, if you have a blown-air torch, reduce the size of the flame a little while maintaining the heat. With a steady hand holding the tongs, apply the solder stick to the top of the joint. If the heat is correct, then the solder will melt on contact with the seam and run down it in a bright silver thread. If the heat is not yet achieved, spin the hearth again and spend a little more time raising the temperature. If and when you need to apply more solder, apply it further down the seam until you are satisfied that the job has been completed.

As soon as the soldering is finished, grip the body with the tongs and cut through the annular rings of binding wire so that no damage is done by uneven cooling and contraction. If any wires have soldered to the joint or are held by borax grip them with round-nosed pliers and with a twisting action roll them off the surface of the body. This should be done when the metal has cooled. After all wires have been removed the body may be placed in the pickle to remove the borax and to clean it.

The second method of soldering involves the cutting of the solder into small squares, perhaps of 2mm side at most. These squares are known as paillons or panels, and on being cut should be deposited in the borax dish. With a pair of fine tweezers you should place the panels along the boraxed joint, perhaps 5mm apart. The body should now be placed on its back, joint uppermost, on the hearth, with pieces of hearth bricks on either side to prevent it from rolling as the hearth is turned. Heat slowly at first, passing the flame back and forth so as not to boil the flux and displace the solder. If any of the solder is displaced you can push it back into place with a long piece of iron binding wire when the flux is shiny. In soldering with panels it is most important to heat both sides of the joint equally; any heat difference will result in the solder running on to the hotter side and not into the joint.

Whichever soldering method you have used, check the joint carefully after pickling, and if the solder is short anywhere, inside or out, you must resolder it. A faulty seam will always break open during subsequent work.

After a successful soldering the joint must be cleaned up and all surplus solder removed. If the joint is in perfect alignment the work is straightforward and is carried out with a file. All lumps of solder must be removed, as well as any in a thin skim that has spread out from the joint. Use your file in combined longitudinal and diagonal movements, so covering the most surface with each stroke. Note the effect of your filing: it is easy to see which action removes the most metal. When you have nearly removed all the solder, modify your action to give a finer surface, ready for the next abrasive.

After filing you must refine the surface further using a water of Ayr stone. Water of Ayr stone is only available from a silversmith's tool shop and it may be purchased in the form of square sticks of several sizes.

You must dip your stone into water and, working as you might with a file, rub and grind the surface, using more water when the surface becomes dry. The stone leaves a matt surface that allows you to see any remaining file marks, which will glint in the light. You will also be able to see any remaining solder, which must be filed away.

If the joint was not completely aligned, then remove as much solder as possible and then mallet the joint over the bar or mandrel upon which the bar was shaped. This will move most of the metal into line, although a ridge will be left both inside and outside the body and only filing can remove it. This is bound to leave the metal slightly thinner in the joint area, and if the joint alignment is poor you really

should cut the joint open and start again.

When all stoning has been completed the area may be refined further with a very fine wet and dry paper or polishing paper, before polishing it. The body should then be placed on a bar or mandrel and, working along its length, malleted as it is rotated, following scribed pencil lines. This will true the body ready for whatever is to follow, planishing or raising.

If the form is to be developed by raising it is most important that you do not try to move too much metal at a time and that when you reach the seam you drive it down on to the stake with the full face of the hammer. Catching the seam with the side edge of the hammer puts it under unnecessary strain and is likely to break it open.

Planishing

Planishing is the smoothing of metal, carried out by systematically hammering it on a suitably shaped and highly polished stake, using a hammer the striking face of which is also highly polished. The general aim of the technique is to remove any deep marks left after raising and finally to true the work around its axis, as well as to develop a surface which is consistent with the aesthetic qualities of the design.

There is a comprehensive variety of stakes upon which planishing may be carried out and which may be obtained from silversmith's tool shops. The simplest stakes, eminently suitable for planishing dishes, bowls and deeper curvilinear forms such as teapots, are called horse's head stakes. Whatever the upper shape of a horse's head stake, it has a tapered square peg projecting from its underside. This

Horse's head stake.

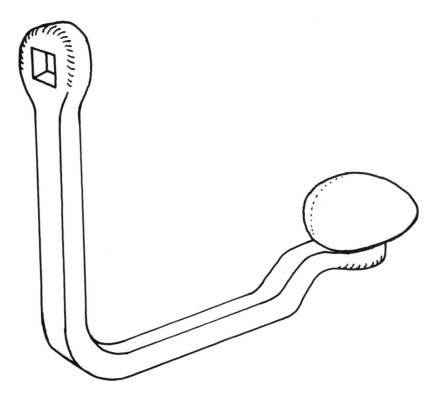

Horse with stake fitted.

peg can be fitted into a horse, which is an L-shaped square bar with a broad section at each end, pierced by a square hole. One end of the horse is also cranked to enable a stake to fit into particular body shapes. Horses have sharp edges around the holes when they are purchased and these should be rounded off with a coarse file or a grindstone. Remember that you must wear safety spectacles when you use a grindstone. Rounded edges prevent damage to the inside of your work and can enable you to planish a smaller piece of work. If you have the use of a metalwork lathe, simple, domed shapes may easily be turned and the peg made square with a hacksaw and file. There are other useful stakes that may be purchased, such as jug stakes, cow's tongue stakes and three-armed stakes.

Some are expensive, but with hard work using a hacksaw and file you can modify steel bars to your requirements. If you know a blacksmith you may be able to get steel bars bent to your specification. Large bolts can also make useful stakes, particularly spoon stakes. As already suggested, a scrap yard or engineering works may prove to be a useful source for odd lengths of bar.

Planishing hammers are stocked by silversmiths' tool shops, and the most useful size weighs, with its handle, approximately 214g (7fioz). It has one round face 20mm in diameter and one rectangular face 23mm x 18mm. When you purchase the hammer the round face will have a flat surface with sharp edges and these should be softened to eliminate the possibility of your making deep cuts in your work if you

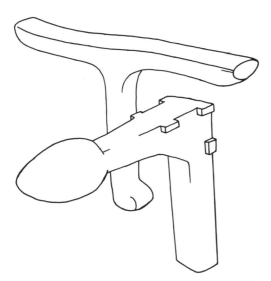

Planishing – jug stake and 3-arm stake.

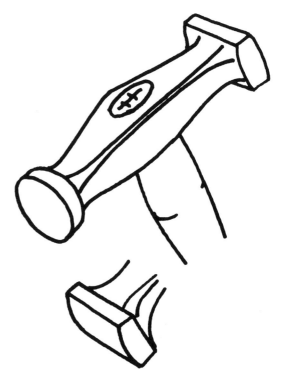

Planishing hammer.

are inaccurate in your hammering. The hammer faces will not be highly polished, but they can be polished with fine wet and dry paper and polishing papers, followed by the use of a polishing motor or vigorous action with leather and a polishing compound. The leather should be quite coarse and thick and glued to a board or stick, with the rough surface uppermost.

The round hammer face is generally used to planish curvilinear forms. The surface of the rectangular face of the hammer is curved on an axis at right angles to the length of the tool. This face of the hammer is used to planish straight-sided forms, such as cylinders or truncated cones. There are also heavier planishing hammers that have a comparatively limited use.

An important category of hammer is that which is used to planish bodies that have concave or flared profiles. Such hammers have curved faces, as on the rectangular face of an ordinary planishing hammer,

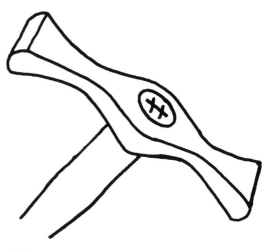

Collet hammer.

but they are more pronounced. The hammer head shafts are also longer than those of a standard planishing hammer so that it is possible to reach into deep, curved forms. These hammers are commonly known as collet hammers.

A crucial task in planishing is the selection of the correct stake. The simplest way of doing this is to place a stake over the side elevation of your design and to assess its shape against the outline of the drawing, or you might sight the stake against the profile of the actual piece of work. You must also ensure that the stake fits the curve of the plan form of your work. The stake must now be put inside the work to check the fit. It must not be too tight a fit in any direction; there should be some leeway. If the fit is too close then the body

will expand as planishing proceeds and lose the designed shape, while too loose a fit will result in a deeply marked interior, a rather ridged external surface and difficulty in attaining a true form.

Before planishing can begin you must decide how the stake is to be held. If you are planishing a shallow dish or a bowl, a horse's head stake can be held in the bench vice by its underpeg. The exact position and angle at which you arrange the stake can be determined by the need to avoid the risk that your work might catch on the vice as planishing proceeds, and also your need to be comfortable as you work.

Stake and hammer now chosen, your work should be annealed and cleaned in pickle and then, using a pair of pencil

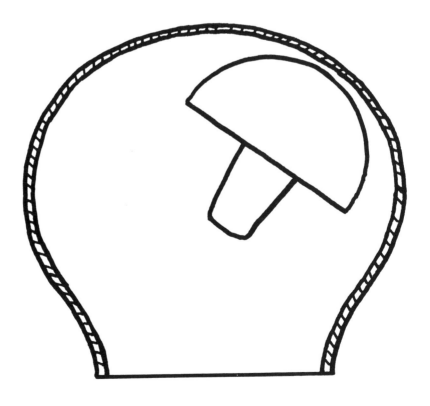

Trying stake inside body.

compasses, the outer surface should be scribed with concentric circles approximately 1cm apart. You then place your work, with the centre point in direct contact, on to the stake. Hold the work in position using your index finger and thumb placed equidistant above and below the point of contact, while your other fingers are loosely curled, with the second finger resting lightly on the surface of the work. Commence planishing by striking the work direct upon the centre point and follow this with a blow immediately above the first and, turning the work continuously, complete a circle of hammer blows. Circle upon circle of hammering should follow, and you should move the

work a little towards you as each circle begins. Each hammer blow and each row of blows is slightly overlapped so as to leave no unworked areas. As the planishing nears the rim of the work the method of holding it will have to be changed to one of gripping the edge between the thumb and the forefinger, using the second finger as a steady. While you have been planishing you may have found that the hammer is not always producing a ringing sound as the work is struck, and, indeed, it may have sounded positively hollow and the metal may have been dented. This is usually because you have not been holding the metal at the correct angle. To ensure that the area that you wish to hammer is in

Planishing in circles.

direct contact with the stake you should press the hammer face firmly upon the metal surface, and so on to the stake, and carry on planishing. The worst situation that may arise is that you have not chosen the correct stake in the first place and thus that you need to start the selection process all over again.

After you have finished your first course of planishing, you should inspect the inner and the outer surface of your work. If your dish or bowl has been formed with the use of a mallet, the surface of the metal will have been comparatively smooth before planishing started and it is just possible, provided that a highly polished stake and hammer have been used, that no more

work will be needed. However, it is far more likely that there will still be a few deep marks made by the sinking or raising hammer or the stake that you have used, and to remove these you will need to anneal your metal and planish it again. With experience you can assess the surface of the metal before the first planishing and hammer heavily enough to remove all offending marks. The ideal, of course, is to raise the metal carefully in the first place and so to leave no deep and damaging marks. Once you have achieved a surface without deep marks you must assess the metal surface once again. You will almost certainly find circular ridges formed by rows of hammer marks and, if not, the

Radial planishing.

hammer marks may simply be too large and clumsy for the character of your design.

To remove circular ridges on your work you must planish it again, but in radial lines working from the centre point. Do not anneal it. It is usual to draw pencil lines from the centre point of the vessel and to use these as a guide for the hammering. When an area between the lines is finished it may be shaded with pencil lines so that you will know when you have eventually covered the whole surface.

In the case of simply refining the size of the hammer marks, scribe new pencil circles on the work and planish it again,

without annealing, and hammering rather more lightly than before. Some people prefer to polish their work between courses of planishing so as to be more sure of what they have done. The ultimate aim of planishing is to produce a surface that is right for the design and that is even and true, with no ridges or runs of hammer marks to impair it.

The general procedures of planishing that have already been described apply to all shapes and sizes of vessel, and it is the type of stake or hammer that will vary. In the case of bowls and deeper curvilinear forms which have compound curves in their profiles you may find that you have a stake with similar curves, in which case you will simply need to change the position of the stake as you planish up the body. To reach into a deeper form you may also need to hold the stake in a horse and you may also need a bottom stake to planish the bottom of the vessel. To do the latter you can use a stake with a long understem or you can use a suitable horse's head stake held in a bottom stake holder or a piece of steel tubing. When you are using several stakes in the planishing of one piece of work it is helpful if you are able to overlap the planishing from one stake to another so that you achieve a smooth transition in the change of profile and avoid unsightly ridges.

In planishing a long, shallow dish, a suitably shaped elongated stake will be needed, and it will be necessary to planish alternately clockwise and anti-clockwise around the body so as not to twist and distort it. It is also possible to work backwards and forwards along the length on either side of the dish. You will again need pencil lines to help you to work accurately. You will be fortunate if a long dish does not distort a little, but careful hand manipulation and pressure against

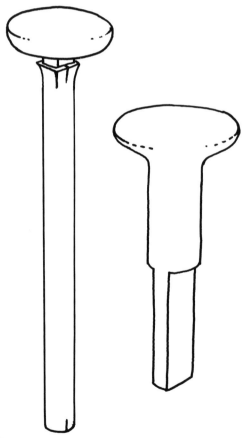

Bottom stakes.

the edge of the workbench can control this.

Very deep forms are planished in the same way as any other form, guided by the scribed pencil lines. Care must be taken that the work is held at the correct angle, otherwise a distortion of the body and a loss of symmetry will quickly occur. It is in planishing deep forms that cow's tongue stakes or stakes that you have made for yourself come into their own. You may also be able to use a stake in a horse, and it is in this case that it is important to have rounded the edges of the horse so that there are no sharp parts that may damage the inside surface of your work. If your work combines a bulbous lower section with straight or concave sides above it you will planish the lower part with the round face of your hammer and the upper part with the rectangular face. The curved rectangular face will produce a hammer mark similar to that made by the flat round face on the bulbous surface of the work, thus giving a unity to the finished appearance of the whole vessel.

If your piece of work is to have a flat bottom with a sharp edge you must take great care in planishing. Planishing a flat surface with close hammering may result in an awkward expansion of the metal to form a pimple or round. This is difficult to control but may be avoided by 'open' planishing. A space is left between each hammer blow and the surface is re-planished in a similar fashion two or three times more, so avoiding any localized stretching. In the case of the sharp edge, it

should be left slightly rounded until the very last minute, so as to avoid any thinning the metal at that point.

If it proves extremely difficult to planish a deep piece of work satisfactorily, particularly in the lower areas, then you might consider cutting out the base so that access may be gained from both ends. Such a suggestion may appal the purist, but to attain perfection of form by any means at your disposal is a reasonable justification.

In planishing a straight-sided form you should work on a polished steel bar of the appropriate diameter. In the case of a truncated cone, if you have a suitable tapered mandrel then use it, and, if the form is seamed, you can work from whichever end suits you. You may please yourself which hammer face to use on a straight-sided form. The round face, which has a flat surface, will make an elongated hammer mark the appearance of which may enhance a straight-sided cylinder. The curved surface of the rectangular face will leave a near circular mark. At this stage it is worth pointing out that a hammer mark may enhance a particular form and produce a texture or an alternative rhythmic pattern. Do not be afraid to experiment, perhaps using scrap metal for trials.

If you intend to remove all traces of planishing and have a sheer finish on your work you must planish it to a very fine and true surface so that you lose as little metal as possible when you stone, file or use abrasive paper to smooth the surface down.

— 10 —

Bending and Folding

This chapter is concerned with the techniques of bending and folding metal by using simple and direct methods of working.

There really is no limit to the type of product that might be designed to exploit some aspect of bending and folding, and combinations of flat planes and curved corners of various radii or flat planes with razor-sharp edges can go together to produce exciting forms.

The most obvious project is probably a box; but that is only a beginning and the techniques may be used in the design and construction of almost any product, from tea- and coffee-pots, to candle holders, dishes or even abstract structures. The techniques may also have a commercial attraction, because used cleverly and creatively they may represent a quicker and therefore a less expensive way of making pieces.

The equipment that is required to undertake the several techniques need be of only the simplest sort, including blocks of hardwood, a variety of steel bars, a boxwood mallet and a bench vice. Articles with sharp corners are constructed with the aid of a scraper made from an old file.

One of the simplest methods of bending metal involves scribing a line on the metal blank to mark where the bend is to take place and then holding it between blocks of hardwood in the bench vice, with the scribed line showing a little above one block. A third block, at least as long as the metal blank is wide, is then used to push

the projecting metal to whatever angle is required, as shown in the illustration. At this stage you may use a mallet to push the metal finally into place. On no account should you strike the metal with the mallet direct. Instead you should strike the wood block, moving back and forth along its length. This will eliminate the possibility that you might make ripples or dents on the metal surface, which will mar its appearance and will take many expensive hours to remove. The radius of the bend of the metal will not be quite constant at this

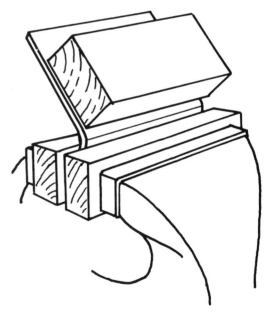

Bending with a woodblock (diagram and photo).

stage, and you should remove the metal from the vice, reverse its position in the wood blocks, put it back in the vice and use the mallet again. The result of this operation will not be a razor-sharp corner but rather a tight, but light catching radius. If you require a slightly larger radius then you can round off the corner of the wood around which you are bending the metal.

A greater radius may easily be obtained by bending the metal around an appropriate steel bar that is held in the vice. Once again, a line is scribed on the metal blank to indicate the centre of the curve that is required. The blank is placed on the steel bar with two wood blocks placed on either side of the line. Using pressure from the palms of your hand on to the blocks, the blank is bent around the bar to what-

ever angle you desire. In bending the metal check the angle when you sense you are approaching what is needed. To go past the required angle and to attempt to bend the metal back may result in awkward hollows in the flat sides. A simple aid to check the correct angle is a template made from metal; this may easily be applied at any stage during the process.

In using the techniques that have been described and in considering the matter of cutting metal blanks it is worth looking carefully at your designs. For instance, the upper profile may not be horizontal, it may have one or more high points or it may be curvilinear in form. It is easy to make a full-size model of your design in wood, plaster, cardboard or even a non-precious metal. The exact profile can be plotted and

Sheet metal about to be bent using a wood block and hand pressure.

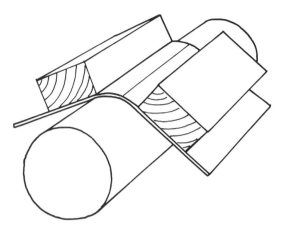

Bending around a bar (diagram and photo).

shaped on your model, from which you can easily make paper patterns for the metal blank, which is cut to shape before you bend it. There are advantages in this plan of action; you can refine your design at the model stage and later avoid awkward and time-consuming work in cutting, shaping, and possibly even damaging the surface of your work when it has been soldered together. Futhermore, if you wish to repeat a design you will have the patterns and model easily at hand.

The size of the corner radius that you achieve when bending metal, particularly between wood blocks, will depend upon the gauge of metal that you are using and also the length of the piece that you are bending. It is a matter of material resistance, but the natural tendency of the

Sheet metal being bent around a metal bar using wood blocks and hand pressure.

94

Form with high points.

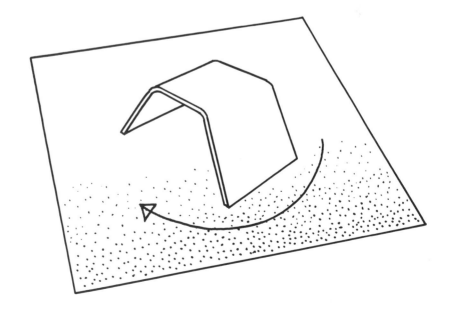

Rubbing down a piece on abrasive paper.

metal may result in a more attractive curve than that which you envisaged, so be prepared to be flexible and to accept the natural properties of the metal. In general constructional terms, metal with a thickness of 0.9mm is ideal, although for very small items you may well use thinner gauges just so long as you pay due attention to the fragility of an object that is extremely light.

The soldering together of the folded or bent components of a design is not unlike the methods described in Chapter 8. Fitting the joints is a simple but important matter. The early stages of achieving a fit can most quickly be done with a file and the final stages by rubbing down the work on a sheet of abrasive paper. The author glues abrasive paper, usually of the aluminium-oxide variety, to a piece of melamine-faced chipboard, which ensures an absolutely true surface. When you are using an abrasive surface you should always work with a circular action and change your grip on the work at regular intervals so as to ensure that you remove metal evenly and do not wear down one side more than another.

If you wish to solder a base plate on to a body you should first cut the plate to the outline size. You can place the body on a piece of metal and scribe round it and, to avoid irritating distortions that may be caused by shears, you can cut the plate to shape with a piercing saw. The fitting edges of the plate and the vessel should be filed to matching angles so that the plate drops into position and the joint occurs exactly on the corner edge and will thus be invisible. The methods of wiring are illustrated.

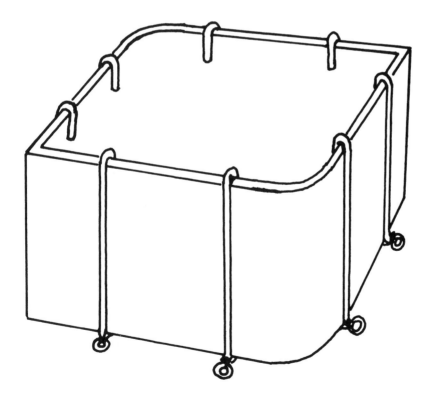

Wiring base to body.

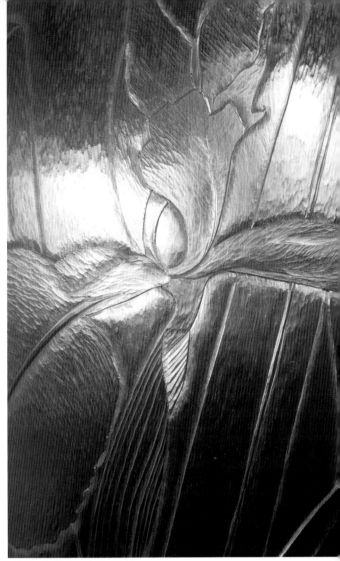

Angus McFadyen: Carved vase showing a
strong sculptural quality. A heavy gauge
of silver was used. Whole vase and detail
shown.

Janina Oliver:
Interlocking condiment
set in silver.

Don Porrit: Silver flagon.

Malcolm Appleby: Bowl Britannia: silver and 18 carat gold beads. 15cm diameter approx. A design which exploits the soft alloy superbly to produce a beautiful fluid surface.

Karin Paynter: Teapot: Silver and ebony.

Karel Bartosik: Card case in silver and gold.

Clive Burr: Noughts and Crosses: silver and slate.

Clive Burr: Enamelled box: Silver-enamelled panel with fused gold leaf and fine gold cloisonné wires, lined with lace wood.

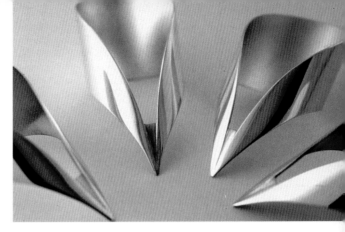

Angela Betts: Silver napkin rings.

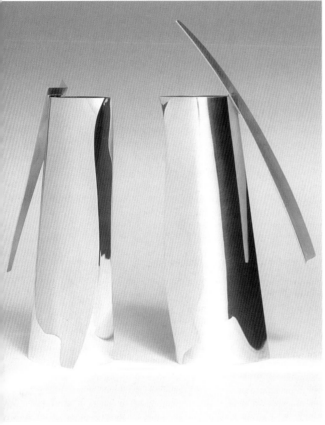

Rebecca de Quin: Hamburg water jugs: Silver and gold-plated. 18cm high excluding handles.

Charles Hall: Magnum claret jug in silver and glass.

*David Bromilow: Cutlery:
Hand-forged with stainless
steel blades.*

*Wally Gilbert: Silver and
gold beaker: Gold is fused to
the silver, a very delicate
and exacting technique.
Photographer Margaret
Ksycka.*

Kay Ivanovic: Silver teapot: Body spun, etched and fabricated. Branch handle.

Keith Tyssen: Mace for Humberside University, made by Alan Mudd. Silver, parcel gilt, rosewood shaft, carved and enamelled coat of arms.

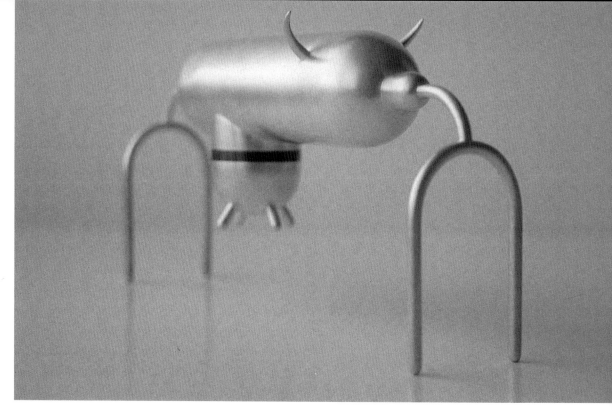

Nigel Turner: 'Cow' cocktail shaker: Silver and steel. 30cm long, 16cm high.
a. The udder is removed to fill with ingredients.
b. The black band acts as a strainer to hold back the ice when pouring.
c. The udder forms a tasting cup.

Chris Knight: Spinning teapot and infuser. Silver
and polyethylene. Private

Base filed to fit body.
Diagram also shows
body wired for
soldering.

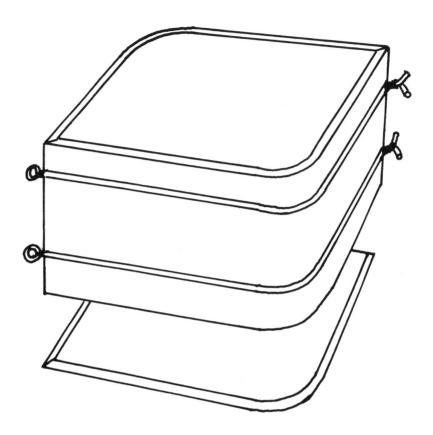

If you are making a box and need to add the lid cover, the fitting procedures will be the same as for the base plate, aiming for an invisible joint precisely on the corner. However, before soldering can take place you must decide where the parting line between the lid and the body will be positioned and this line must then be scribed on the body with a metal scriber using either a straight edge or a scribing block. You must now cut a slit with a fine saw at some point along this line, usually at a corner or on a curve, as shown in the illustration. This allows air to leave the box as it is heated for soldering and to re-enter as it cools. The wiring of the body before soldering is shown in the illustration. When soldering is completed the box must

be allowed to cool and must not be put into liquid, and most certainly not into pickle, before the lid is cut off with a saw. The scribed line may be obscured by oxide after soldering and should be scribed again so that you can saw the lid accurately. After the lid and the box are separated you should rub them down on an abrasive surface to true and smooth their edges. The fitting of wires and design variations of lid and box fittings are described in Chapter 11.

In making a box with sharp corners, and particularly a square, rectangular or any other multi-sided form, you can use just one piece of metal from which to form the bottom and the sides.

The equipment that is required is

97

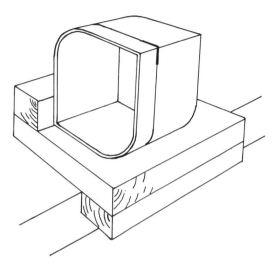

Slit cut prior to soldering top on.

uncomplicated: a flat piece of hardwood or a similar material that will accept wood screws, at least eight round-headed screws, a G cramp and a scraper made from an old file. A flat or half round-file 20cm (8in) or 26cm (10in) long will be the easiest to hold while you are working, and the scraping point is made from the handle tang. The tang must be heated until it is red hot and then bent round to a right angle at a point 13mm (fiin) from the tip. The tip should then be filed or ground to a shape that will scrape a vee-shaped groove in sheet metal. Remember to wear safety spectacles if you use a grindstone. The cutting tip must be hardened and tempered so that it will be hard enough to work without quickly becoming blunt and yet not be so hard that

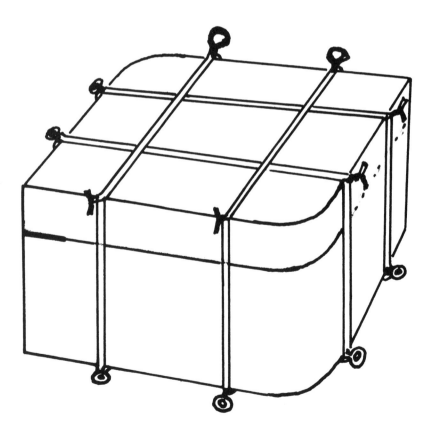

Wiring the top plate before soldering.

*Half round file
made into scraper.*

it is brittle and liable to fracture. To temper it, heat the tip to red heat and quickly quench it in cold water, which will harden it, and then brighten the surface with abrasive paper. With a small flame, heat the tang at a point about 13mm from the cutting point. The tang will change colour as it is heated and bands of colour will creep towards the cutting point, changing from pale yellow, to straw, to yellow brown, at which point the scraper should be quickly quenched in cold water. After a final sharpening on an oilstone it is ready for use.

The blank of metal, comprising the base plan with all the sides laid out around it, must now be marked out, using a tri-square, dividers and a metal straight edge, all lines being deeply marked with a sharp metal scriber. This must be done with extreme accuracy, especially if you are making a box without a hinge, because the lid will have to fit in as many different positions as there are sides.

The blank must now be fastened to a piece of wood or some other flat material by means of round-headed screws, two at each corner, with the heads overlapping

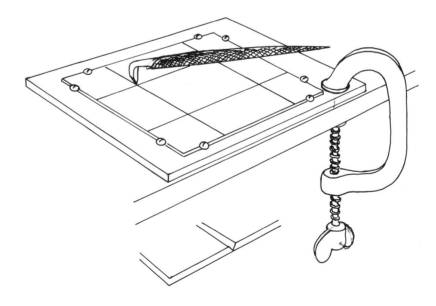

Scraping box.

the edge of the metal. Fasten the wood block to your work bench with a G cramp as shown in the illustration, which also illustrates the blank laid out with scribed lines.

Use both hands to hold the scraper, one gripping it near to the cutting point to apply a downward pressure, while the other grips the far end and draws the scraper along the scribed line. Place the scraper point into a scribed line at the far side of the blank, apply a little downward pressure with the forehand and pull the tool towards you. Do not attempt to remove a large quantity of metal quickly with excessive downward pressure, because the tool will almost certainly deviate from the scribed line, leaving an unsightly gash. If this does occur you must turn the board round and continue to scrape the groove

from the opposite direction. If all goes well, scrape all the grooves, in rotation, to a shallow depth and then start again to work more deeply.

Do not scrape all the grooves in one direction to the full depth and then attempt to scrape across them from another direction because the scraper will dig into the metal at the intersection and make holes just where you do not need them. Carry on scraping until you sense that you are in danger of cutting right through the metal and then remove it from the wood base and inspect the underside. If there is a ridge on the reverse side of each groove then you need scrape no more, and with a piercing saw you can remove the unwanted pieces of metal at each corner of the blank. Use a fine flat file to true the angles of the sawn edges that are

Bending a scored joint.

to become the corners of the box. You can now bend each side into position using hand pressure, holding the blank in both hands and pushing against a flat surface, as in the illustration.

If you have not cut deeply enough not only will the metal be reluctant to bend but it will not form a sharp corner and the side edges will not meet properly to make a good solder joint, so do not be too impatient with your scraping!

In soldering the carcass of the box the wiring is straightforward: a wire is wrapped around the sides with loops at three corners and the ends twisted together at the fourth. This arrangement allows for an even tightening all around the carcass and eliminates any chance that the wire may cut into the corners. The vertical corner joints and the inside joints between the sides and the bottom of the carcass must now be boraxed and the piece placed on a flat surface on the soldering hearth. The hearth should be rotated and the carcass heated with a large, all-enveloping flame. A small, hot flame will cause the metal to twist and distort. When the required heat has been reached solder should be applied at each corner and, as it flows along the joints, the flame should move with it, drawing it along. Heating into a vessel is not always easy because the flame may blow back, and it is worth directing it along the length of each inside joint that is being soldered.

When the soldering is complete the vessel should be allowed to cool naturally because to quench it would be to warp it. When the top is added the procedures are exactly as have already been described earlier.

— 11 —

Wire and Tube

WIRE

Wire in one form or another is absolutely essential to a silversmith. Its uses may be divided into three categories.

First, it may be used for purely practical and mechanical purposes such as the thickening of the edges of boxes and their lids and the making of the bezels for the fitting of lids.

The second category is where the wire fulfils a practical function but is visible and prominent and contributes to the aesthetic impact of an object. For instance, a dish might require a reinforcement to its edge, and, if it is oval in form, the wire might vary in width and lend emphasis to the quality of the curves. In a tall design the body might comprise two separately made forms and at their junction a wire might provide architectural emphasis while concealing the joint.

The third category is where wire is used purely for decoration. It might be applied to a vessel in straight, wavy or spiralling lines or in any other form that can be imagined, including stylized representational images. A silver object might also be embellished with gold wire, and wires can also be hammered so that their width varies, perhaps to give emphasis to a curvilinear rhythm. Wire may also be woven for decorative effect.

Silver and gold wire may be obtained in a wide range of dimensions and sections, including round, half-round, square, rec-tangular and triangular. Your dealer in precious metals will have a listing of all the most popular available sizes and sections and should be able to supply you with any length that you request.

Generally speaking, the most popular and appropriate wire for thickening the edges of boxes and other containers measures 3.2mm x 1.6mm, while the usual dimensions for a bezel wire for lid fitting are 6.4mm x 1mm.

If you are working in base metals, such as copper or gilding metal, the situation is quite different. The range of wires is restricted, there are hardly any suppliers who will consider selling short lengths and the cost will be comparatively high. To make thickening wires and bezels it is possible to cut strips from a sheet of metal.

You can make your own wires from basic stock if you have a draw bench and draw plates. However, even the simplest draw bench is expensive, as are draw plates. With such a variety of wires so easily available, and in whatever length you require, a drawbench is a luxury except in a busy group workshop. A draw plate for small-diameter, round wires may be useful for making pins to secure handles or for making core wires for small hinges. If you are to do this you will also need a large pair of pliers or a pair of hand draw tongs that may be purchased from a silversmith's tool shop. Square wire may also be made and reduced by using specialist hand-operated rollers. These will also reduce sheet metal in thickness. They are expensive but useful.

Malleting wire.

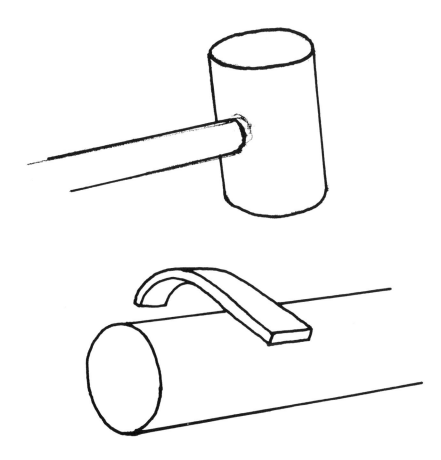

The equipment that is required for bending wires is not at all complex. Wire may be bent over steel bars and tapered mandrels with the aid of a Tinmans mallet or a horn mallet, and also by using hand pressure. Other wires may be bent in slots in hardwood by using hand pressure. Sharp-cornered bends can be achieved by filing vee-shaped cutouts before using hand pressure. Pliers of various sizes are also useful, but should be used with care because the jaws may easily mark the surface of the wire. It is possible to buy pliers with a parallel closing action, which will cause the least damage to the metal surface.

To bend a wire into a circular or oval form you should use a steel bar or tapered mandrel, held in the vice, and a Tinmans mallet or a horn mallet. First calculate the amount of wire that is needed. In the case of a circular form, measure the diameter of the circle, multiply it by 3.14 and this will give you the length of wire that you need. In the case of an oval you might work around the plan with a pair of dividers set at a known measurement. If you are fitting a wire into or around an oval vessel you can wrap a sheet of thin card or stiff paper around the inside or the outside and mark the point at which it overlaps.

Having cut the requisite amount of wire,

103

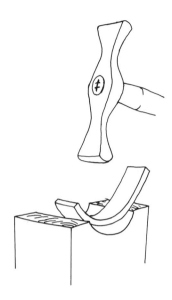

Hammering heavy wire into wood.

it should be annealed and each end malleted around an appropriate bar or mandrel. If it is reasonably light wire, the bending can be completed by using hand pressure, but if it is heavy then you will have to use the mallet. A heavy wire can also be bent by driving it into a hollow cut into wood and using a collet hammer.

While bending the wire around the bar or mandrel you should at regular intervals place it on a metal plate or some other hard, flat surface and, turning it all the while, strike it with a Tinmans mallet to prevent any twisting or distortion of the plane of the circle or oval.

When the wire is shaped it should be checked for size on the vessel to which it is to be fitted. If it is oversize overlap the ends and saw through the overlap to produce a

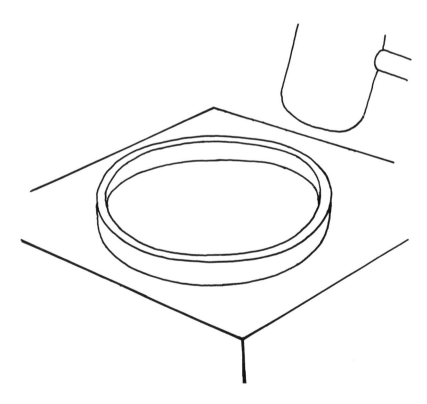

Malleting ring on steel plate.

joint that will require only a minimum of filing. It is not necessary to make an absolutely true circle or oval before soldering, but make sure that the line of the joint flows reasonably and without a sharp kink. It is not absolutely necessary to use binding wire when soldering a wire joint. Instead you should spring the joint ends past each other and carefully pull them back to meet each other, when they will hold in place under a sprung pressure. You should then borax the joint and place the wire flat on the hearth. Heat the ring at a point opposite to the joint and, when it is red hot, work the heat round to the joint, moving the flame from side to side. You must get each side of the joint equally hot before applying your solder from a stick, unless you have used a preplaced paillon. Use enamelling or hard solder.

It is often necessary to make a ring from a flat wire that is bent in a horizontal plane. You must not attempt to do this with a mallet around a steel bar because the wire will twist, collapse and be damaged. You should cut a slot into the end grain of a piece of hardwood that is approximately 15mm (⅝in) deep, and this slot should be slightly wider than the flat wire. With the wood held in the vice, slot uppermost, one end of the wire is inserted into the slot, and, with hand pressure pushing sideways, the bending commences. The wire will not do as you wish, will distort as you work and you will have constantly to true the flatness of it on a metal plate, using a Tinmans mallet. Carry on with the bending for half of the length of the wire and then start to

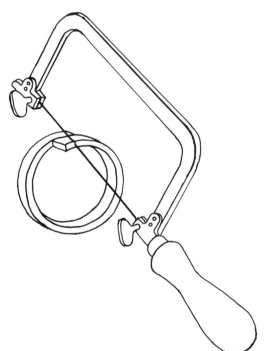

Cutting joint on overlapped circle.

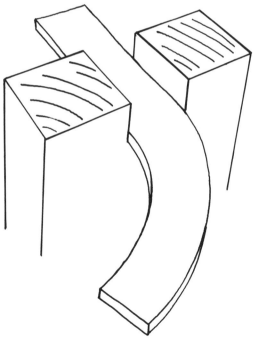

Wire bent in wooden slot.

bend it from the other end. It will be difficult to bend the extreme ends of the wire, so it will be best to use rather more than you need, overlap the ends and cut through the overlap to make the joint. You will almost certainly not work the wire round into a finished form in one operation, but may need two or three sessions, bending, malleting flat and annealing. Soldering will be a similar operation to that already described, and once soldered it will be possible to undertake a careful truing operation with a mallet on a mandrel or whatever stake fits into the form. In the case of an oval you may need two stakes, one well rounded and another more gently curved.

To fit a flat wire on to the top edge of a vessel you should file the fitting edges of both the vessel and the wire to matching angles so that the joint occurs exactly at the meeting point of two planes.

You may need a wire to fit a conical vessel and in such a case you should first bend the wire to match the edge line of the plotted development of the design. Plotting the development is described in Chapter 8 on seaming. After curving to the developed arc the wire can be bent conventionally around a tapered mandrel.

Wires may also be applied to vessels whose top profiles rise and fall in an even or irregular manner. In such a case the development must be plotted before any metal bending begins. This may easily be done by inserting a roll of stiff paper or thin card into the vessel and drawing around the top edge, on to the paper. The paper can then be laid out on the bench and the wire bent to follow the drawn line,

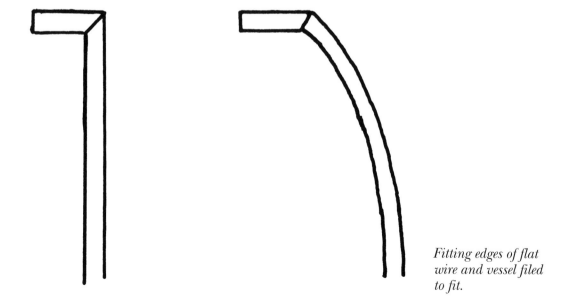

Fitting edges of flat wire and vessel filed to fit.

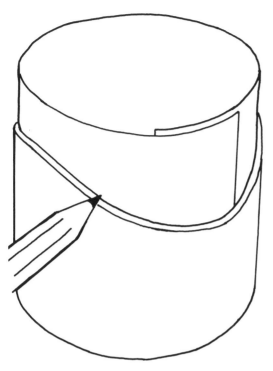

Drawing development of a 'wavy' top.

using a slot in wood. Once the wire has been bent accurately to match the development it may be bent in the other dimension to become circular and to fit into the vessel.

It is always necessary to put at least one wire into a box; this is the bezel wire, over which the lid fits. You can also fit thickening wires into the box and the lid, and a bezel wire into the box alone. The last suggestion looks good and strong and also allows you to line the box and the lid with leather or cloth to give a luxurious quality to the product. Thickening wires are usually rectangular, 3.2mm x 1.6mm, while bezel wires, also rectangular, measure 6.4mm x 1.5mm. These wires should be stocked by your silver dealer and be obtainable in any length that you specify. There is a variety of arrangements for wires and lid fittings in boxes of all shapes and these are illustrated as sections.

Wires made to fit into boxes that have a combination of bent corners and sharp corners are made by the methods

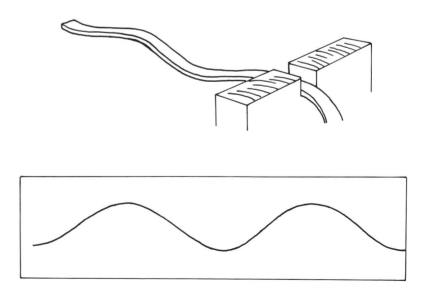

Development laid out – wire being cut.

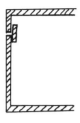

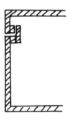

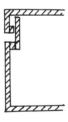

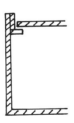

Various sections of boxes.

described in the preceding chapter, using wood blocks and, or, hand pressure to achieve the required shape.

In fitting a thickening wire or a bezel into a square or rectangular box you might imagine that it is best to calculate the total length of wire that is required, bend it in three places and complete it by joining the ends. In practice you need only to make small errors in filing any of the three angle joints to make accurate fitting impossible. Instead, cut two pieces of wire each a little longer than half the total length that is required. Mark where the bends are to take place, and at these points make vee cuts with a square or triangular file, very nearly cutting right through the metal. You can now bend the wire with finger and thumb pressure to produce a sharp corner angle, which should be immediately soldered with enamelling solder. One wire should now have its ends cut and filed square to fit tightly into the box. The ends should then be mitred and the complete process that has already been described carried out on the other wire so that it too fits into the box.

At this point it is necessary to describe the process involved in soldering wires into boxes, or, indeed, into any vessel where a thickening wire is required.

First, you must clean the area in the box where the wire will be soldered into place. You now scribe a line around the inside of the box, representing the depth to which the wire will fit, so that if you are using wire 3.2mm wide the line will be scribed this distance below the metal edge. You should now take an engraving tool and cut a line in the metal, starting near the top edge of the box and pushing a curve of metal in front of the tool, stopping when the scribed line has been reached. This process must be carried out at least twice on each side of the box. The small curls of

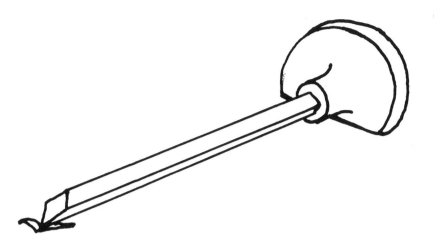

Cutting a stitch.

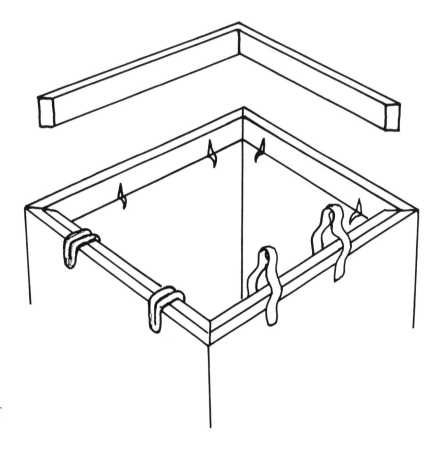

*Fitting and holding
thickening wire.*

metal standing proud of the surface are called stitches, and when the thickening wires are lowered into place they will rest on the stitches and will not fall into the vessel during soldering. The wires are held in close contact with the sides of the vessel using split or cotter pins, or clamps made from binding wire. The process of fitting and holding the wire is shown in the illustration. The wire is soldered into the box, after cleaning it and boraxing all fitting surfaces, with hard or medium solder,

depending upon what grades have already been used. It is a good idea to preheat the hearth before soldering and to use a large flame, kept low, and moved back and forth as the hearth is turned. The wire is slight in bulk and will heat up more quickly than the box, become red and expand away from the box sides, which may result in an impossible joint. Your aim is to heat the wire and the box to the same temperature at all times. The processes that have been described are also used in making and

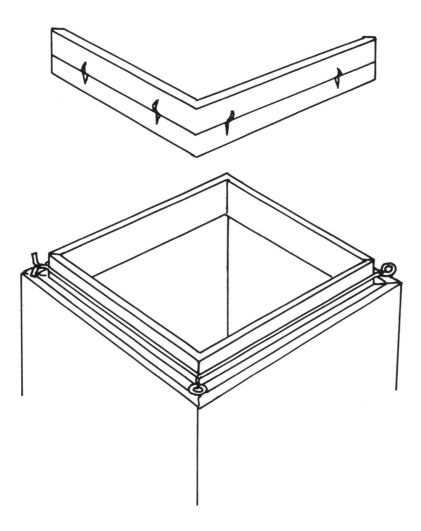

Fitting bezel into box – bezel wired.

securing thickening wires in the lid of a box.

As already suggested, a bezel is best made from wire measuring 6.4mm x 1mm, as offered by your silver dealer. It should be made in two pieces, like a thickening wire. When the wires are fitted to the box, the ends must be checked with a tri-square before they are mitred to form the joints. This will ensure that the bezel is absolutely true and that the lid can be put on to the box without lengthy and tiresome adjustment, nor that it will be too loose in its fit. The bezel is also prevented from slipping during the soldering process by the use of stitches. A line is scribed to represent the level of the edge of the box, and the stitches are cut up to the line on the surface that will be soldered into the box.

Lids rarely fit on to boxes immediately after soldering; there may be an excess of solder in corners or slight deviations in the line of the bezel or the lid, but with patience and the careful use of small riffler files and water of Ayr stone a close fit can be achieved. Pay great attention to your filing technique so as not to lower the corners of the box or leave grooves where the edge of a file has cut into the metal. Common-sense techniques such as filing with a diagonal movement away from a corner joint and the use of a straight edge to check levels will save you much time and frustration.

As suggested in the introduction to this chapter, wires may be applied to a surface as a decoration. The exact form of decoration is, of course, very much a personal matter and so it will be based on a source of reference or a theory that appeals to the designer. It is not a form of decoration that is used extensively, but there are a few exponents who achieve extremely sensitive results. Generally speaking, one would not expect to achieve a mirror polish between

wires, the soldering and cleaning up operations make that unobtainable. However, if you wish to have a polish, then a soft hand polish, with the use of an oxidizing agent alongside the wire can offer an extremely attractive appearance. You might also experiment with satin finishes achieved through the use of fine abrasives. Wire may also be used in conjunction with other forms of decoration such as chasing, a technique that is described in Chapter 13 on decoration.

The holding of wires in position while they are soldered is obviously of vital importance. On cylindrical forms a series of binding wire circles should be satisfactory. On truncated cones or curvilinear forms a solution to that already described in wiring seamed bodies should also be satisfactory. You will need to turn your work as you heat it with a large and all-enveloping flame, bringing it to heat slowly so that the wires do not get too hot too soon and possibly melt or expand disastrously before the solder melts. In soldering wires for decoration it might be possible to apply the solder at one end, and it should then follow the heat along the boraxed joint. Another method would involve the placing of paillons of solder along the length of the joint. If this type of decoration appeals to you, then it would be sensible to produce some small, purely experimental pieces in the first place, or to start with very small articles and slowly build up your competence, confidence and appreciation of the aesthetic possibilities.

Another possible use of wire and tube (dealt with in more detail below) is the cutting of short lengths that can be soldered to a metal surface to stand vertically and form a relief decoration. There are a number of possibilities in this sort of decoration, from using an organic source of reference such as wood end

111

grain, to building an area of sections of different heights and diameters in a seemingly random pattern, to an architectural or engineered approach where great geometric accuracy and discipline are involved in arranging the elements of the design.

In producing these types of decoration, the area to be decorated should be boraxed and the solder should be melted on the area by using paillons of solder so as to retain control of the amount of solder on the surface. When the metal has cooled, the elements of the decoration, lightly boraxed, should be arranged, and the whole area heated until the solder runs and all the elements of the decoration have been secured. With this sort of decoration you should not be considering a highly polished background, but rather a matt or an oxidized surface.

To produce a highly disciplined and geometric decoration is extremely exacting and in terms of the time required an expensive undertaking. The surface to which the decorative elements are attached must be accurately marked out, but by far the most serious factor is the prevention of the decorative elements from moving during the process of soldering. A method by which this can be achieved involves the drilling of the back of each element of the decoration and soldering in place a small peg. Holes may then be drilled in the body of the piece to be decorated and the element of the decoration pushed into place. Extremely small paillons of solder may now be placed inside or outside, on the back or the front, of the joints to be soldered. A large flame and a slow build-up of heat until the solder runs should now follow. In finishing a piece of decoration like this it is unrealistic to expect a mirror polish, rather you should consider a satin or an oxidized surface. Should the area of decoration be sunken, as in the top of a box perhaps, it might be embedded with coloured resin.

TUBE

The use of tube relates to wire in more ways than in decoration, and in the production of hinges the combination of tube and wire is inseparable. Over a much broader range, your silver dealer will stock a wide variety of tube sizes, ranging from napkin-ring size to several finger-ring sizes. In smaller sizes, tube with thinner walls can be obtained at diameters ranging from 12.7mm down to 0.76mm. It is also possible to obtain joint tube from hinges with diameters ranging from 6.35mm to 3.15mm. This type of tubing has a thick wall that, besides giving strength to a hinge, allows you to make a flush hinge. You can also obtain square tube varying in size from 12.8mm to 3.15mm in diameter, and also a limited range in an octagonal format. Your dealer will supply you with a catalogue or information sheets listing precisely what is available.

If you are working in base metals such as copper or gilding metal you may be able to obtain high-quality brass tube that is suitable for hinges from a model engineering or model aircraft shop.

The wide variety of silver tubes that are available from stock removes the need for you to fabricate any for yourself, and, in any case, because of the power and the energy required, the task cannot be realistically undertaken without a drawbench.

The availability of larger sizes of tube opens up the possibility for the designing of exciting structures with tubes as the main components. The accurate joining of tubular components is an exacting process, and crisp architectural qualities must not be lost. You can ensure that a tube registers accurately with the one to which it is to be soldered by inserting a collar or bezel into one before the joining operation. Another device for ensuring an appearance of great accuracy can be used when a structure is secured to a flat surface. The fitting ends of the tubular structure can be finished with flat sheet bases inserted into them, to which are attached threaded spindles. The flat surface, to which the structure is to be attached, metal or other material, is drilled in the appropriate places and the structure secured by nuts. If you are securing your structure to sheet metal this method removes the need to clean the joints, which will certainly leave light-catching dimples and ripples, and also will allow a much simpler and safer polishing operation.

One of the prime uses for tubing is in hinges and these are to be found in boxes and tea- or coffee-pots, to name some of the more obvious examples. For the average box, tea- or coffee-pot, a joint tube with an outside diameter of 3.95mm should be quite adequate, while for small boxes for rings and other small items of jewellery an outside diameter of 3.15mm is ideal.

Perhaps the simplest example of a hinge is to be found in a box, and once the basic principle of construction is understood then a little thought will supply the solution to other projects. In making a hinge for a box, the side upon which it is to be situated must have lengths of 3mm-square wire soldered into place in both the box and the lid instead of the thickening wires and the bezel that are to be found on all sides of a box without a hinge. These square wires are known as bearer wires because they will bear the pieces of tube

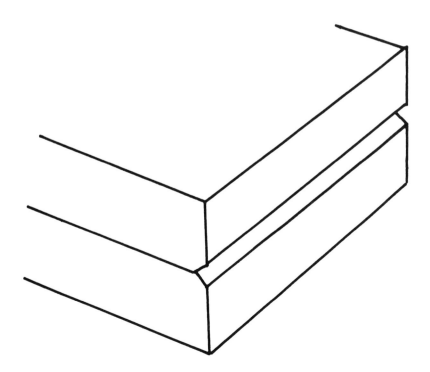

Filing bevels on box and lid.

113

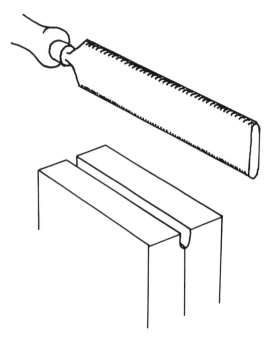

Deep slot cut with round edge joint file.

that will constitute the hinge. The bearer wires should be soldered into place before the thickening wire and the bezel wires on the other three sides of the box and the lid. As in other solderings, stitches can be cut to prevent the bearers from slipping below the edges of the box and the lid, and split pins or binding-wire clips used to hold the wire tight to the soldering surface. When the bearers and all the thickening wires and the bezel are in place, and the box and the lid fit absolutely perfectly, you can start to consider cutting a channel in the bearers which will hold the lengths of tube that will constitute the hinge. These lengths of tube are always known as the knuckles of the hinge.

It is usual for a lid to open up to a 90-degree angle or very slightly more, and to achieve this the hinge tube should be sunk into the bearer to a depth of slightly more than three-quarters of its diameter. In starting to cut away the necessary amount of metal from each bearer you should first file a bevel on both the box and the lid edges. The total width of the two bevels should be no more than a quarter of the circumference of the hinge tube, as shown in the illustration. Holding the box

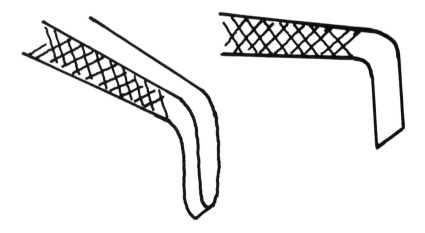

Scraper made from old file.

and the lid tightly together you should now cut a narrow groove, the width of the bevels, down to a depth of three-quarters of the diameter of the hinge tube, as shown in the illustration. You cut the groove by using a round-edge joint file, which is a flat file with teeth on only the rounded edges. Another method involves using a scraper made from an old square file, and it is also possible to buy from a silversmith's tool shop a round parallel file which is 3.2mm in diameter. It is essential to cut a groove that is of an even depth along its length, and scribed lines along the face of the bearer wires will help you to gauge your accuracy. You can also use a thin straight edge, placed in the groove, to detect any tendency to rock on a central high spot. If you have a high spot work only on that point with the scraper or the end of the file. In such circumstances, a round jewellery riffler file may also be useful.

Once you have made the narrow groove, you must work on the lid and the box separately, and cut away metal until the lid and the box can be clamped tightly on to the hinge tube, ready for the soldering that will complete the hinge. You are at this stage undercutting, as illustrated. You must work consistently, taking the same amount of metal from both the lid and the box. In the later stages you may feel that you are very close, but cannot decide where to remove metal. If you clamp the tube in place and twist it, it will be marked by the high spots, which will indicate where you must remove more metal from the bearer.

Once you are satisfied with the fit of the hinge tube you must decide how many knuckles you will want in the box. It is always an odd number and the minimum is five: three on the box and two on the lid, always the greater number on the box. The knuckles should be cut with a fine saw, very

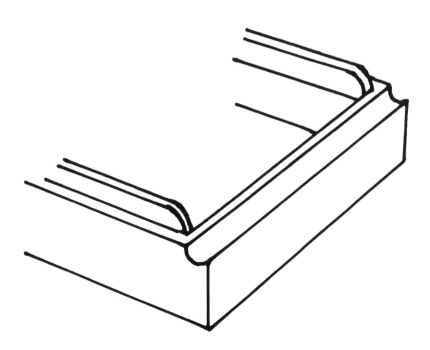

Cutting metal from box and lid.

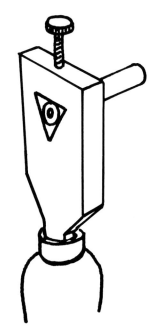

Joint tool for filing knuckle ends.

slightly oversize, and each end must be made absolutely true so that when the hinge is complete only the finest of lines will indicate any divisions. You can true the ends of the knuckles with the aid of a special joint tool, available only at a silver-smith's tool shop. The knuckle is placed in the tool, the end projecting fractionally, and then filed flush with the face of the tool. You can also true a knuckle by placing it in a pin vice which is spun in your hand while resting against the bench; the end of the knuckle is then lightly filed with a fine flat file. The file must be held at right angles to the axis of the spinning hand vice. The two outer knuckles should be left a little oversize and allowed to project beyond the sides of the box.

All the knuckles should now be placed in position in the box and the divisions between each knuckle marked with a

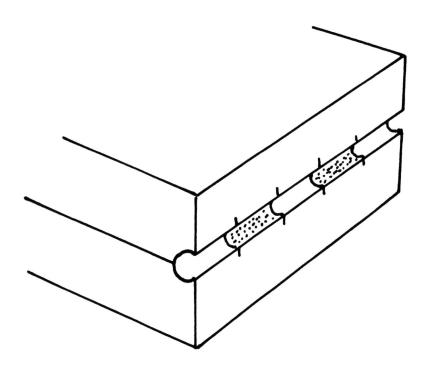

Box bearers boraxed and pencilled.

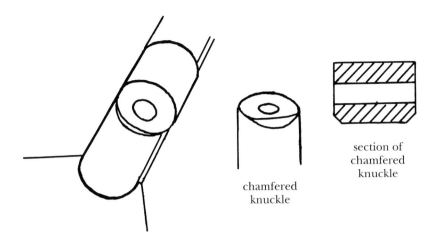

Knuckles chamfered and shown positioned in the bearer.

chamfered
knuckle

section of
chamfered
knuckle

pencil. Now the knuckles should be removed and pencil lines drawn across the bearer channel to delineate the divisions between each knuckle.

The area where a knuckle will not be soldered to a section of the bearer channel should be now pencilled black, as should any fitting surfaces of the box and the lid. Where knuckles will be soldered to the box or the lid the surface should be carefully painted with a thin solution of borax. The bearer channel will now resemble a

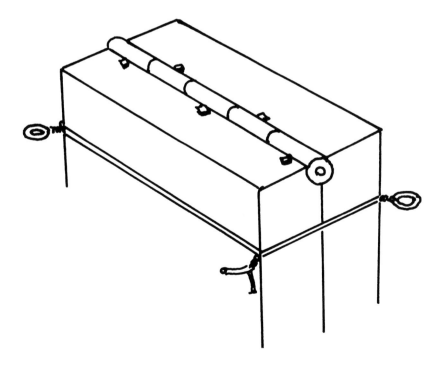

Box hinge ready for soldering.

117

chequer board, with boraxed areas enabling solder to secure a knuckle to the lid or the box, and pencilled areas discouraging solder.

Each knuckle is now slightly chamfered at each end for about a half of its circumference, excepting the outer knuckles that are chamfered at one end only. The knuckles may now be placed into the bearer channel of the box. Those that are to be soldered into the box should have the chamfers positioned over the boraxed area, while those that are to be soldered into the lid will have the chamfers positioned so that they will coincide with the boraxed areas in the lid channel. The lid

should now be placed in position very carefully, and the lid and the box wired together with binding wire, with loops at three corners, and the ends twisted together on the fourth. Place the box on the hearth, hinge uppermost, and dab a minute blob of borax at the centre of each knuckle where it is to be soldered to either the box or the lid, and add a small paillon of solder.

You should now heat the box with a large, gentle flame, turning the hearth all the time. You may increase the heat while watching the paillons of solder very carefully. Your aim is to just melt them so that each knuckle is just secured to the lid or

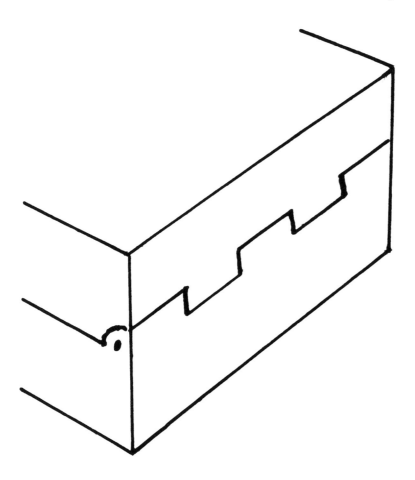

Flush hinge.

the box. At this stage you do not want the solder to run freely in case it attaches adjoining knuckles. The box should be allowed to cool and the lid and the box parted; they must not be pickled. The knuckles in both the lid and the box may now be separately fully soldered using paillons of solder and more borax. Do not be over-generous with solder, or you will have fillets of solder at each end of the knuckles, although the chamfers that you cut are designed to prevent this from happening. If you have used a joint tube with a thick wall, then that area of the hinge that projects beyond the side of the box may be carefully removed with a fine flat file to produce what is known as a flush hinge.

The principles of hinge making that have been described may be applied to hinges on all types of vessel, including round ones, such as tea- or coffee-pots. It is all a matter of where the bearers are situated. In a teapot the hinge might be incorporated in or above the handle socket. On a circular box it might be designed to project, to match a thumb catch at the front. It is really a matter for you to think about, balancing aesthetics and technical necessities, but at all costs avoiding the impression that the hinge has just been stuck on as an afterthought.

— 12 —

Miscellaneous Forming Techniques

There are vital areas of metal forming which are not difficult to grasp or master if experience and confidence have already been built up in practising sinking and raising in particular, although the ingenuity developed in folding and bending is also invaluable.

The first area to be considered is the production of spouts, handle sockets and spoon bowls. In each of these there is a common factor, and that is the problem of estimating the blank of metal from which to form the item, and the common solution is to make an accurate model from which measurements may be taken. Models may be made from strong cardboard, sheet metal or Plasticine. They may also be carved, sawn or rasped from wood.

Spouts and handle sockets or hollow handles can be adequately constructed from metal with a thickness of 0.9mm or greater, if you wish. The tools that are required include collet hammers, raising hammers, doming hammers and mallets. A pair of dividers is essential. The metal can be worked over a variety of stakes, from small saddle stakes to small jug stakes, or quite simply small lengths of steel bar that you modify for yourself. You will also find that a variety of pieces of wood are most useful, particularly hardwoods such as holly or box or even very old oak. It can be hollowed and grooved for hammering metal into it or shaped more

like a stake. In a workshop with a generous floor area, a length of tree trunk can accommodate a series of hollows, deep and shallow, and many useful grooves around its circumference.

To estimate blanks for complex duo-curve forms like spouts is not as straightforward as to estimate for a raising, and you will need an accurate model as an aid. Before you even start to make a model you should have finished the body of the vessel and established the level of the lid opening. It would be helpful if the base were also attached so that the alignment of the spout may easily be checked.

The first stage in making the model is to cut a template that represents the side elevation of the spout. This can be done by taking a tracing from your design and transferring it to strong cardboard or sheet metal. When it has been cut to shape, attach it to the vessel with two lumps of Plasticine and check that it looks as you hoped it would on paper. Check also that the pouring lip is slightly higher that the highest possible level of liquid in the vessel when it is standing on a level surface.

If all your requirements are satisfied then begin to model the spout, rolling pellets of Plasticine between thumb and finger and gradually add them to the model to complete an accurate form. In the final stages put the model into place on the body of the vessel and make sure

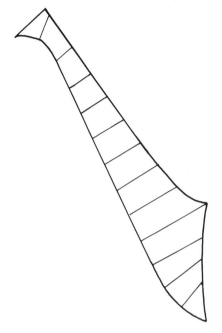

Side elevation of spout model.

Marking spout model.

that it is perfect in form and proportion.

To make a simple estimation of the blank let us assume that the spout has a D-section, that is, a rounded under belly and a flat or nearly flat upper surface. It is the under belly for which a development is needed if it is to be made easily and accurately. The metal or cardboard profile in the centre of the model provides a vital datum line along which you should mark a series of consecutive numbered points, each 1cm apart. The edge of a straight metal strip or ruler should be pressed into the model at each point in turn and, with a rocking motion, a line is marked in the Plasticine and at a tangent to the profile from which it arises.

On a piece of paper you now should draw a vertical line and divide it with horizontal lines spaced at 1cm intervals and numbered like those on the model. At point number 1 on the model measure with a pair of dividers the diagonal distance from where the impressed line arises from the datum line to where it terminates at the top edge of the model. Mark this measurement on line number 1 on the drawing, first on one side of the datum line and then on the other. Repeat this procedure at every numbered point on the model, and transfer all the measurements to the drawing. Finally join all the marks on each side of the datum line, and you will have a line drawing of the development of the underbelly of the spout.

Take a tracing of the development and use it to plot the blank of metal, either by sticking the tracing to the metal or by pricking a series of marks that can be linked. Cut the blank and trim the edges accurately and anneal it. Now scribe a

121

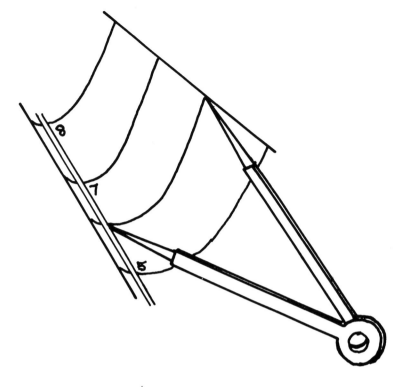

Measuring model.

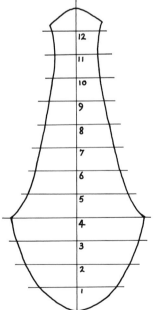

Development of spout.

centre line on both sides of the blank so that you can check for accuracy during the forming operations.

You will now need a collet hammer and pieces of wood in which channels and hollows may be cut. First cut a shallow channel in a piece of wood and with the collet hammer drive the metal into it, using the scribed line to guide the accuracy of the hammering. To ensure complete accuracy in the cross-section you should work the metal from alternating sides of the scribed line. As the blank is wider at the bottom you will need additional rows of hammering at that point. You can cut the channel in the wood a little deeper and work the blank into a deeper form, and you can also lay the blank on the bench, first on one side and then on the other, and tap along its

*Hammering blank
into wood block.*

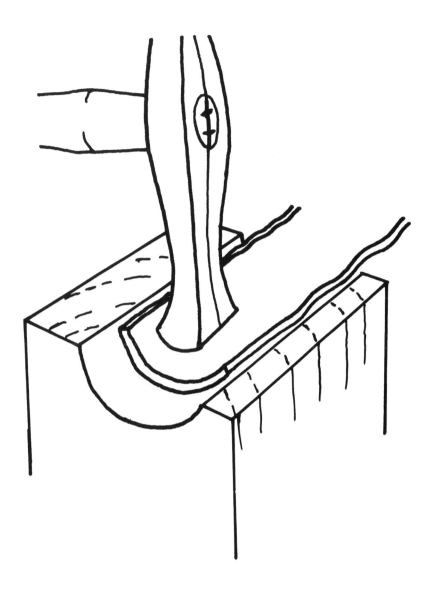

length with a horn mallet, which will also narrow it. You may be able to push the wide lower end in using a horn mallet over a metal stake. As you work the form will certainly twist, but by pressing the narrow top end, edges down, on to the bench and twisting the bottom end by hand the twist can be eliminated. As with any operation, the metal will work-

harden, and you should anneal it regularly. You should also work slowly because rash hammering may cause inaccuracies that will be difficult to correct.

As the blank is narrowed to the required diameter, you must consider the other dimensions. The lower end of a spout often curves in to meet the body to which it will be attached and, at the top end from

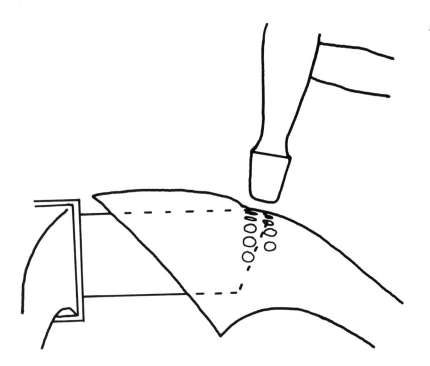

Raising spout.

which liquid pours, the side elevation displays a concave curve.

To shape the lower end of the spout you can use a raising hammer and a suitable stake. You can easily establish where raising should begin by holding the metal form over your design drawing or by comparing it with the model. You can also make a card template to use as you work. Mark the proposed work area with pencil lines and start raising a very small amount to one side of the central datum line and, moving across, gradually increase the amount until the line is reached, when you will carry on, gradually raising less metal until you reach the pencil line. You should then move back across the spout and so on until the bottom edge is reached. Working backwards and forwards across the spout will lessen the chances that a severe twist may occur, but the spout sides may open up with each

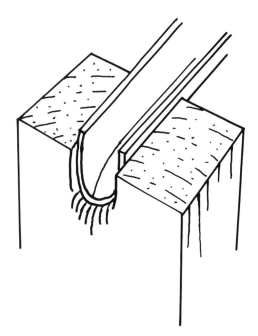

Curving spout tip in deep wooden channel.

Working spout lip on curved piece of round bar.

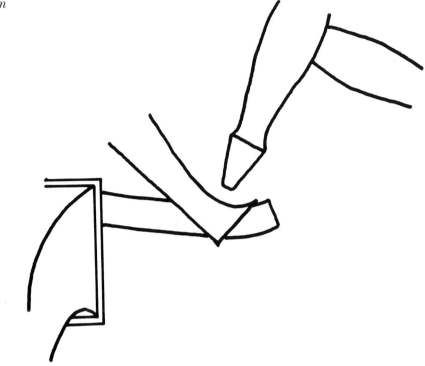

raising and require pushing into place again, after annealing, but before more raising.

To shape the pouring end of the spout you will require a collet hammer with a thin head that can reach into a narrow channel. If you decide to modify a hammer on a grindstone remember that you must wear safety spectacles. You should round one end of the channel in the piece of wood in which you have shaped the spout, and then hammer the tip of the spout around it.

The channel in the wood should be deep because the sides of the spout will try to open out. This process puts the metal under great strain and so it should be annealed regularly. You can also work on the spout on a curved piece of steel rod and hammer on the outer surface. It is also

possible to shape the lip by fine raising, particularly in the case of a teapot, because the spout may not be as slender as in a coffee pot.

You may have designed a spout that has an egg-shaped cross-section or a circular section and in such a case it is possible to fabricate a conical form and to raise inside and outside curves to arrive at the final form. This is an extremely exacting proposition, although at some stages filling it with pitch and working on a sandbag could be helpful. The author prefers to plot a development for the underbelly and another for the upper surface, form the underbelly first, trim it accurately and then form the upper surface and file and fit it to the underbelly.

Whatever the form of a two-piece spout, it is in essence a tapered form and so the

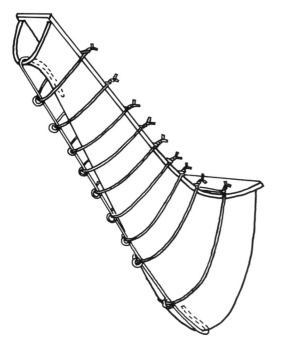

Spout wired for soldering.

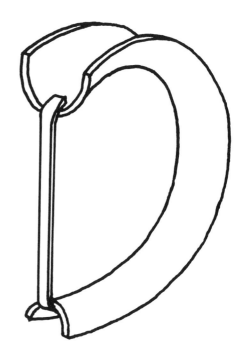

Hollow handle blank – soldered strip.

wiring before soldering is carried out in a manner similar to the wiring of a truncated cone. You should use the hardest possible solder, enamelling, to eliminate any possible running of the seam when the spout is applied to its body.

When you have fitted the spout to the body of the vessel that you are making, it will, of course, be necessary to solder it in place. You should first secure it to the vessel with two pieces of Plasticine. Now check that it is vertical by using a tri-square and, when you are satisfied with its position, scribe round it on to the body of the vessel. Cut stitches all around the scribed line, having cleaned the area which will be soldered. You will already have drilled the body with a grid of holes no more than 3mm in diameter. The author believes that the more holes in the body

that allow liquid into the spout, the greater the pressure of liquid and the better the pouring performance.

Soldering can be a delicate operation, and the vessel should be propped on its back on the hearth so that the spout is near to vertical. At the bottom of the spout it may be possible to push the stitches over the edge of the spout, like jewellery claws for stones. It may also be possible to run binding wire around the lower part of the spout and the body of the vessel. Cautious heating will be needed, followed by your chosen method of applying solder.

You can make hollow handles in the same way as you make a spout, creating a model first, and estimating the development. As you work a handle it tends to spring apart and it is possible to solder a

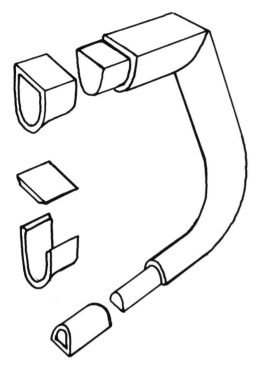

Handle sockets – one exploded to show construction. Handle shaped first.

strip of metal in place to prevent this from happening.

If you are making the sockets for a handle it is a good idea to make the handle first and then to mark the socket's fitting areas on each end of it. The areas on the handle which will fit into the sockets should be filed away to allow the sockets to fit flush with the surface of the handle. A socket would normally be made from metal 0.9mm thick. If the sockets flare into the body form, then they should be modelled in Plasticine on the handle and while it is attached to the body. A development is then plotted for each socket; these are made using techniques that have already been explained. When the sockets have been made they should be put on to the handle and introduced to the body. Any alterations or fitting work should be carried out and then a line should be scribed on to the body around each socket. Stitches can then be cut from under the joint area and up to the scribed line. If the vessel is laid on its side on the hearth,

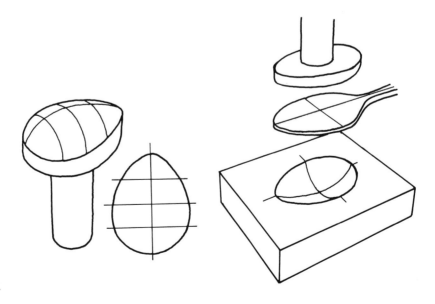

Spoon bowl making.

the sockets may be put into place after the joint area has been painted with borax. You may find in this case that paillons of solder provide a safer soldering system than the use of a stick.

Spoon bowls may be formed by using sinking techniques or by using a doming hammer to form them into a hollow carved in wood. However, if you wish to produce sets of spoons it is much more sensible to make an accurate spoon stake and to stamp the bowls into a mould of lead. A spoon stake may be made from a large bolt head or shaped on the end of a steel bar. It is also possible to buy spoon stakes that may be modified in shape. If you are to use a lead mould you may be able to obtain a block of lead, otherwise it must be melted in a suitable receptacle. The hazards associated with the melting of lead were described in Chapter 3. The spoon stake may be driven into the lead when it is cooled, using a

heavy hammer. Alternatively, an accurate mould may be carved in hardwood. The development for the blank of the spoon bowl may be plotted on the stake and, when cut and annealed, the blank is simply placed over the mould and driven down with a heavy hammer. Before stamping you should mark the longitudinal axis of the mould together with the cross axis at the widest point, so that you can place the blank accurately. You should not need to undertake any planishing, but you may need to adjust the edge of the bowl to achieve a level plane.

You may stamp a spoon bowl the bowl blank and handle of which have been forged from a single bar of metal, and it is therefore timely at this stage to consider forging in general.

Forging is carried out with the aid of collet hammers and the curved stretching face of a raising hammer, depending upon

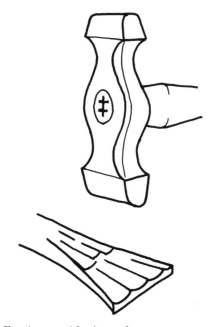

Forging – widening a bar.

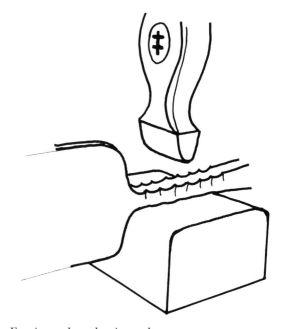

Forging – lengthening a bar.

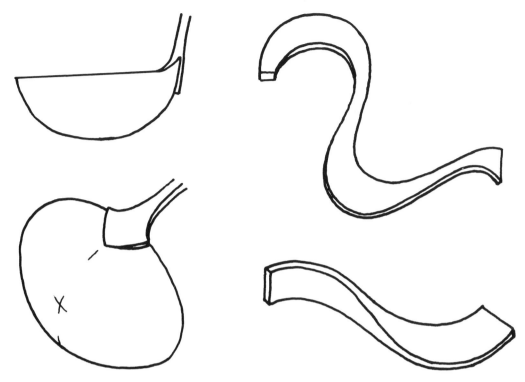

Bowl and handle made separately.

Decorative curved shapes forged.

the scale of the forging that you wish to undertake. The metal to be forged will usually be worked on a curved surface, such as a stake held in a vice or on the upper surface of a heavy raising stake.

Round bar is the most suitable section of metal for forging. It is easily moved in any direction without any real problems, whereas, with square bar, the face not being hammered tends to become concave and may be difficult to deal with.

Quite simply, if you wish to widen a bar you hammer it with the curve of the hammer head and the curvature of the stake in line with its axis, while if you wish to lengthen a bar you hammer it with the handle of the hammer in line with the axis

of the bar. There is no easy formula to tell you what size of bar is needed to achieve a particular dimension or form, only experience can help. However, it is possible to widen a bar to form the blank of a spoon bowl and then to stretch it to form the handle. After forming the bowl blank you should reduce the handle a little at a time, otherwise it may become far too long. You may find that it is preferable to make the handle and the bowl separately and to solder them together, possibly with the handle extending on the underside of the bowl. At all times when forging it is necessary to work systematically, it is no good hammering a bit here and a bit there, because once a forging is out of control

129

it is difficult to retrieve the situation.

Forging can be used to produce a variety of attractive forms, such as sculptural bases and intriguing handles. It can be used to accentuate curves in wire, so that widened areas lend emphasis to the rhythms of a design. Once you have understood the principles of forging then only your imagination will limit your exploitation of the technique.

— 13 —

Decoration

Surface decoration is an anathema to many designers, and yet to others it is the means by which they stamp their personality upon their work. In theoretical terms decoration can be used to lend emphasis to particular forms, and inter-esting contrasts can be achieved by setting decorative areas against plain metal. Some techniques can be developed from small experiments on scrap metal, while ideas for other categories of decoration may require research among reference sources

Punched decoration – two punches overlaid.

and hours of development work with pencil and paper or on a computer.

STAMPING AND PUNCHING

This is an extremely simple technique that can be practised on silver, gilding metal or copper. The punches can be made from steel rod and easily shaped with a file, and the punching face can be left with file marks to provide texture. The clarity and impact of a punch mark may depend upon the thickness of the metal that is to be decorated and also on the size of the punch. Metal that is 1.3mm thick will allow for a deeper and more significant impression than metal which is only 0.9mm thick. A punch with a large face will meet with far more resistance than one that has a small face.

Interesting surfaces may be made by overlapping two differently sized and shaped punches. The actual arrangement of the punch marks may also relate to the form on which they are displayed, a radial arrangement on a circular disc, for instance. You may have seen interesting textures in nature, in rock or in rotted wood grain, which can form the basis for designed decoration. You can also design extremely disciplined, well-spaced architectural decoration that will require careful and accurate work. Punched deco-

Illustration showing pitch bowl, chasing hammer and tools.

132

ration may be enhanced by the use of an oxidizing agent which will provide an illusion of greater depth. You should not expect to polish an area of texture to a high degree, although you might burnish high points. Punched decoration often looks at its best on a domed surface.

CHASING AND REPOUSSÉ

The techniques of chasing and repoussé are complementary and have in common the use of pitch and a wide variety of steel tools similar to punches. Generally speaking, chasing is line work on the outer surface of a vessel whereas repoussé is the action of giving decoration relief by pushing the metal up from behind or inside the vessel.

The pitch is generally contained in a semi-circular, cast-iron bowl, although it may also be held in a wooden tray that you can make for yourself. A cast-iron bowl may be bought at a silversmith's tool shop and in use it stands in a wooden supporting ring or a collar. The author has made a collar from a piece of plastic plumbing pipe 11cm (4.3in) in diameter and 3cm (1.2in) high. A visit to a local building site may provide what is needed! The cast-iron bowl is semi-circular so that it may be tilted to allow you to work at a comfortable angle.

The pitch can be purchased only at a

Illustration with work on pitch. Two tracers in front. Pearls at front of container. Note the design of the hammer; nothing else is suitable.

silversmith's tool shop in quantities of 3kg (6.6lb), so if you know others who would like to practice the art it could be worth getting together. The pitch as bought is too hard and brittle and must be mixed with other ingredients so that it will give where metal is pushed down but will support the surrounding metal. There are several recipes for suitable mixtures; one consists of 6 parts of pitch, 6 parts of plaster of Paris, 1 part of resin and 1 part of linseed oil. However, one tool supplier sells pitch and tallow, and in that case tallow may replace linseed oil. With experience people naturally vary the recipes according to the results that they get. To mix the ingredients you must heat the pitch gently in an old pan or cast-iron cooking pot and add the other constituents slowly while stirring the mixture all the time. The heat should be applied under the container and in a well-ventilated space or in the open air. When the mixture is complete it may be poured into the cast-iron bowl, which may have stones in the bottom to save pitch, or into your wooden tray. Remember that hot pitch is dangerous and if you get it on your skin it may cause severe burns and be difficult to remove. A safe method of transferring it to other containers is to let it cool and harden, and then chip lumps with an old sharpened file or an old chisel. The lumps may then be melted by passing a gentle flame across them. The same method can be used to fill a vessel whose exterior surface is to be chased, and you can also insert a strong stick of wood. If the wood is held in a vice it will allow the vessel to be chased easily. Do not burn the pitch or overheat it because it will lose the qualities that you need.

Chasing and repoussé tools can be purchased at a silversmith's tools shop, but if you prefer to do this, buy only a few essentials in the first place, because you can easily and cheaply make your own, as and when you need them. The basic tools are tracers, which chase lines, and pearls, which are oval-faced to planish the surface of the metal. You will also need one or two domed tools for repoussé work and one or two matting tools which are invaluable for textured surfaces and cannot be made easily. If you make your own tools you will need square steel rod 4 or 5mm in diameter, and a tool will need to be 10cm long. The tool should be tapered a little at the end which is hit with a specialist chasing hammer; this is available only at a silversmith's tool shop. The corners of the square rod should also be slightly chamfered. The working end of the tool will naturally vary according to the work that it is to be undertaken. A tracing tool should be forged to make a shape similar to a miniature cold chisel, except that it will not cut the metal but will push it into the pitch. The working straight edge of the

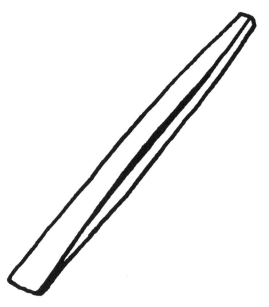

Chasing tool, a tracer.

tool should be rounded, as should the corners, and then it will be polished. A pearl, or planishing tool, will be shaped to an oval section, the face will be slightly domed, the edges rounded and then you should polish the working surface.

There are several ways of applying your work to the pitch. Filling a deep vessel has already been described, but you should also fill a shallow dish or bowl before putting it on to the pitch bowl or, if it is too large, on to pitch in a shallow tray. If you are chasing on sheet that you wish to remain flat, then you might use a piece of metal larger than you need, perhaps with the corners turned down and embedded deep into the pitch. If the metal does warp it can be flattened by using a hardwood punch. To attach your work to the pitch, heat the pitch and push it into a mound using a large, cold metal stake, and then press your metal into place with a piece of wood. The hot pitch will spread outwards, eliminating any pockets of air. If you find that the metal gives and sounds hollow as you work it you must remove it and reset it.

You can mark your design out on your work in whatever manner suits you best, but, as the metal will be annealed and will have a matt surface, it should be easy to see what you are doing.

To commence chasing with the tracer you should hold it between your thumb and first three fingers; the third and the fourth finger will brush the surface of the metal. Lean the tool away from you very slightly off vertical, resting on what you might term the heel of the tool. Now strike the tool with quick but not heavy blows and, with help from your hand, it should move towards you in a smooth action, leaving a clean, smooth, indented line. If you leave a dotted and uneven line you may be leaning the tool too far backwards and you must simply practice to improve. The tracer should move round curves, although for a tight radius you may need to make a tracer with a shorter working length.

You may produce a design that depends upon the sole use of line, although in the interests of variety and emphasis you will

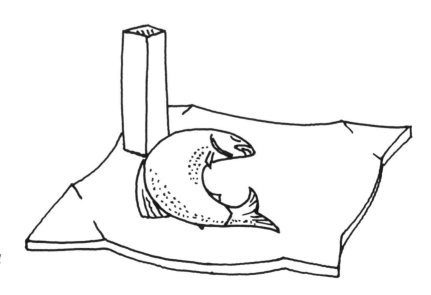

Hardwood punch to flatten metal around a chased image.

certainly have to chase some areas more than once, to produce a deeper or wider line on a curve, for instance. However, chasing a line will almost certainly result in a slight depression of adjacent metal, which means that you are on the verge of a low relief design. You can therefore work over the surface adjacent to the line using the pearl or planishing tool and model the metal into a subtle relief. You must move the tool smoothly while tapping it gently, following the contours that you wish to emphasize. Planishing marks may cleverly represent a quality of the image that you are chasing rather than becoming an absolute reproduction. This might be true, for instance, in the chasing of the form of a fish, where planishing marks of the most appropriate size might evoke images of its scales.

If your design involves more than a little relief, then you must push the metal up from the back surface or from the inside in the case of a deep vessel. This is the action that is known as repoussé. It is usual to first delineate the area of the design by chasing a line around it. The metal must then be removed from the pitch, by using a pair of long-handled tongs, after heating it gently. In the case of sheet metal or a shallow bowl or dish, you can continue to hold it in the tongs and, using a gentle flame, allow as much pitch as possible to run and drip out into your pitch container. In the case of a deep form, you may be able to hold it in tongs or you may be able to devise some method of hanging it by using binding wire. You must heat the vessel very gently, passing the flame backwards and forwards. To use too much heat is extremely dangerous, particularly with a vessel with a narrow neck. With too much heat the pitch in the body will become very hot, expand and spurt out in all directions, including horizontally, endangering anyone close by.

The pitch will eventually slide out of the vessel into your container.

When no more pitch will run off the surface, you can heat the metal to the annealing temperature, burning the residue until it glows with bright spots. When you remove the flame the spots turn grey-white, and, if you quickly quench the metal in cold water and then pickle it, the surface should be near to clean. Any stubborn coke may be removed by using a bristle brush and abrasive powder or steel wool impregnated with soap.

Sheet metal should now be returned to the pitch, but with the chased lines face down in the pitch. The chased lines will show on the metal surface as soft ridges and within the area bounded by the ridges you should use a punch to push the metal into relief. If you find it difficult to judge the depth, push some Plasticine or clay into the hollow, and, on removing it, you will be able to judge the relief. Remember that in punching the metal you are stretching and thinning it, and. if you push too hard and too fast, you may make a hole in it. In fact, because of the reflective qualities of metal it is not necessary to achieve to great a relief. The reflections and the play of light and dark give an illusion of greater relief than actually exists.

In the case of repoussé on shallow dishes you are likely to view the interior and so you can proceed as for a sheet of metal. With a deep form the problem is quite different because you have to reach into areas inaccessible to the hammer and the punch, never mind your hand. In this case we use a tool called a snarling iron that you will have to make for yourself. You will need a steel rod 1cm in diameter and 50cm (20in) long. It should be bent at a right angle 20cm (8in) from one end and at the other end it should also be bent at a right angle, in the same direction as the

20cm length, but at 3 or 4cm (1.2 or 1.6in) from the end. This end should be rounded and polished. The 20cm length should be held in the vice so that the other end is vertical, and the hollow vessel should be placed so that the polished end of the tool rests on the interior of the area to be

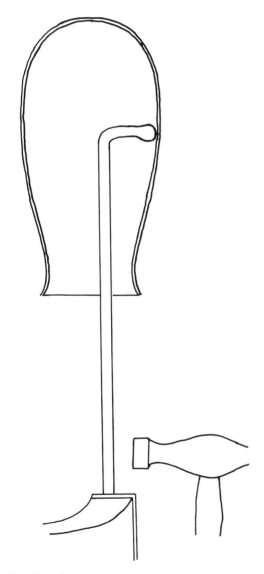

Snarling iron.

raised in relief. The metal rod should now be hammered close to the vice, using a heavy hammer. This will cause the rod to vibrate and the polished end of the tube will push the surface of the vessel into relief.

Following repoussé your work must be annealed and then filled with pitch and the detailing can begin on the outer surfaces.

ETCHING

Etching is a method of decoration which requires no skilled metalwork technique, although, as with all decorative techniques, an ability to draw, design and visualize is invaluable. To actually produce the decoration on the metal it is coated with a resist and the design is scratched or scraped away to reveal the design as bare metal. The metal is placed in a bath of etchant that eats the metal away.

In the past nitric acid has been recommended for this purpose, but it is extremely dangerous, and if handled carelessly may inflict dreadful burns. The associated fumes are also very corrosive and so you should on no account use it. There are safe alternatives, and for silver you can use ferrous nitrate and for copper you can use ferric chloride. These chemicals may be purchased from the suppliers listed in Chapter 16, although you may be able to obtain small quantities through your local chemist. The iron salts will be in crystal form and should be mixed in a ratio of one part of chemical to four parts of water. There is a tendency for these chemicals to stain your hands brown and so you should wear waterproof gloves when you handle them. Although these are 'safe' chemicals if properly handled, they should be kept well away from children, and a doctor or a hospital should be contacted immediately in any emergency.

The ideal modern resist is water-soluble acrylic block ink that can be obtained from the specialist supplier listed in Chapter 16. It is a 'new-generation' product that is used extensively by fine art printmakers. Traditional resists have included bitumen, whose fumes are out of favour with the health and safety authorities. The soluble acrylic block ink can be applied by brush or roller, and crimson is the best colour to work with. When it has dried, it can be scratched or scraped away to reveal bare metal, ready for etching. If you are etching a flat plate it is best done with the areas to be etched placed face down and resting on plastic wedges. This will allow the etched residue to fall away and the etching solution to work most efficiently. The depth of the etch will need to be assessed at regular intervals, together with the impact of the overall image. Different layers of etching may be achieved by etching so far, and then applying new areas of resist, before more etching. Common sense will decree how you position objects other than flat plates in the etchant – a cylinder vertically, for instance. You can, of course, etch right through metal if you wish. An etched design has a special rough and bitten surface and does not have the precise outlines of other systems of decoration, and you will obviously consider this in the light of your design.

FLAME-BURNT METAL

You can texture silver by heating it to beyond the annealing temperature and watching it carefully as it becomes shiny and puckers and almost melts on the surface. The metal should be heated lying flat on millboard or on a heat-reflective block. When the heat is removed, the silver has a grainy, speckled appearance and will have warped a little. It will be black with oxide, but the tips of the grainy texture will polish a little if you wish. Because of the small scale of the texture and the warpage of flat plates, you may feel that only small pieces of metal can be used, but there is no reason why you should not produce a 'mannered' design that exploits warpage. Flame-burnt metal with its oxidized texture may well provide an interesting ground on which to apply wire or shot which will gleam and catch the light.

Shot may be made by melting a scrap of silver or gold in a slight recess in a charcoal block or a piece of barbecue charcoal. However, if you have millboard on your hearth, forget all about charcoal, because it is just as good and lasts longer. You should make a slight depression in the millboard, place your silver or gold in it and melt the metal with a small, hot flame. When it is molten it forms a shining sphere; the heat should then be removed and the shot dropped into a shallow dish of pickle. Perfectly spherical shot cannot be produced larger than 2mm in diameter.

To solder shot to an object place it with a minimum of borax and a tiny paillon of solder alongside. Use a large flame so that the shot does not become very hot before that to which it is to be soldered.

SAW PIERCING

Piercing holes to a predetermined design is another form of decoration, although it has to be said that holes alone on sheet metal constitute a relatively boring and undistinguished embellishment. Piercing is far more interesting when it is used in conjunction with chasing, applied sheet or wire, or engraving. Engraving is delicate and easily damaged and should always be carried out when the piercing is complete. You can mark the areas to be pierced in whatever manner you prefer, and drill a small hole at the point at which you wish to begin piercing. Sometimes an area to be pierced may be too complex to work from one hole and you may need to work back to the starting point because of the width of the metal, or you may be unable to swing the frame of the saw in order to change direction.

Piercing saws are available in two sizes, those that can cut to a depth of 75mm (3in) and those that can cut to one of 145mm (5.7in). They can also be obtained with adjustable frames, allowing shortened blades to be used. Saw blades are obtainable in a range of sizes, from 6/0 at the finest, to size 4 at the most coarse. Generally speaking, size 3/0 is the most useful and will cut metal from 0.9 to 1.3mm thick. Thinner metal can be cut with blades size 4/0 and 5/0.

To position the saw blade, hold the saw frame horizontal, resting against the bench, and fasten the blade into the jaws at the top of the frame, with the teeth facing the handle of the saw. This will mean that, as you pull the saw downwards, the teeth cut the metal. Pass the saw blade through the hole in the metal and slide the metal up to the end of the blade that is already fastened. Now fasten the other end of the blade in the jaws by the handle, while pushing the frame against the bench. The result will be a blade held under pressure and taut. A slack blade will break easily, although one which is too taut will do so as well.

Most piercing is carried out with the work supported by the bench pin; the saw should be kept vertical and you should not force the blade along. You can lubricate the blade by wiping it with the palm of your hand. If you wish to change direction in a curve, simply swing the frame of your saw. However, to cut a sharp corner, to the left, for instance, press on the right side of the blade and continue working it and slowly turning the frame, making room for the

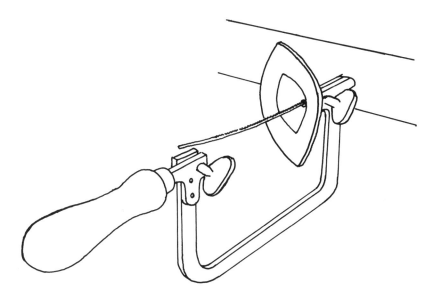

Saw piercing.

teeth of the blade to be able to travel in the required direction. An expert piercer will not require to use a file afterwards, and, if you are able to work with patience and a relaxed grip on the saw handle, you can do the same.

APPLIED SHEET

The application of sheet metal sections to a surface may also form an interesting decorative technique. As ever, it is the exact form of the image and its shape that are important, whether it be varying widths or flowing rhythms. The spaces between applied sections are also just as important as the shapes of the applied pieces.

Soldering comparatively narrow sheet sections to flat sheet should not be too difficult. Surfaces to be soldered will be cleaned and boraxed, and engraved stitches and binding wire used to keep everything in place. The binding wire may be pushed down around the edges of the applied pieces using your thumb nails. Solder can be applied from one end, and should follow the heat and the borax. Applying sections to hollow bodies will inevitably be much more exacting and you may use mallets and stakes to do the necessary shaping. If you wish to apply a large piece of sheet, the solder may well not run right across the joint, even though it may look sound around the perimeter. If there is any air trapped it may show itself as a bulge during subsequent heating operations. In such a situation it may be better to pierce a hole in the back plate before soldering the applied pieces. A joint margin of 3 or 4mm should be adequate.

It is unrealistic to plan a high polish between applied pieces of sheet and so a mixture of soft polish and oxidation will

not only be more realistic but far more interesting.

ENGRAVING

Engraving, which involves the cutting away of metal with a tool to produce a fine vee cut, is a demanding and skilful craft. The result has much in common with a fine pen and ink drawing in aesthetic terms. The line may vary in depth and width, and has a wonderfully crisp and taut quality that catches the light superbly. Without any doubt, an ability to draw is essential in designing for engraving. Anyone who wishes to engrave would be well advised to seek out a good course at a college of art or at a university faculty of art and design.

MOKUME GANE (WOOD GRAIN METAL)

This section has been contributed by Alistair McCallum, who is an expert in the art of *mokume gane* and has an international reputation for the quality of his work.

This technique has been practised for some 300 years in Japan and involves the bonding of copper, copper alloys and silver by fusion. The technique that I am going to explain is an adaptation of the technique using hard silver solder. There are many different methods but this is the one that I favour. I select the metals to be soldered together for their compatability in terms of malleability and ability to be silver-soldered. These would normally be copper, copper alloys, silver and gold. I use copper, gilding metal and silver.

- Cut the metal into strips no more than 25mm (1in) wide. The length of the strip may vary according to requirements, but for small objects 75 to

*Mokume bevelled
edge.*

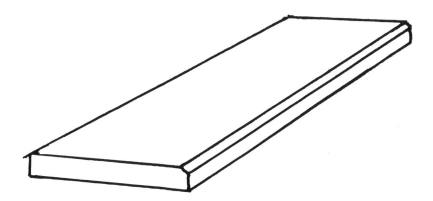

100mm (3 to 4in) is adequate. Try to use as a thick a gauge of metal as is available; I use material 1.5 or 2.0mm thick. The combination of comparatively small sheets with great thickness will minimize the surface area to be soldered but will allow the block to expand into a large sheet when it is rolled out.

- Mix borax with water until it is of a creamy consistency.
- Flatten and then file the surface of one strip of metal so as to remove all oxides, pits and deep scratches and then file a bevel along one long edge of the

filed surface. Paint borax on to the filed surface and repeat the described process on the next strip. Once completed, scrub and rub the metal surfaces with a paper towel to remove the borax and to make absolutely certain that there is no trace of grease on the surfaces. Treat the surfaces again with borax and place the two strips face to face, with bevelled edge to bevelled edge.

- Bind the two strips together with reasonably heavy binding wire, taking care to space the binding wire loops evenly.

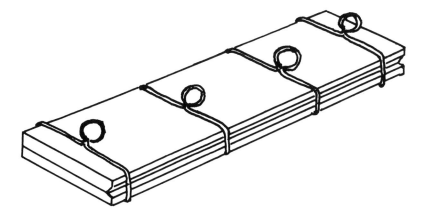

*Mokume – two strips
wired together.*

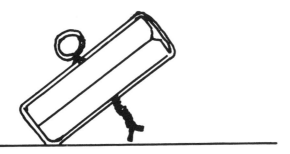

Mokume, resting on twisted binding wire.

- It is important to leave a twisted tail of 5mm on each binding wire loop because this will hold the metal strips at an angle and make soldering much easier.
- Solder only two sheets together at any one time, so that you have only one area upon which to concentrate and so minimize the risk of missing any part of the area.
- Use hard silver solder all the way through the process because this will

allow you to use lower melting point solders at a later stage.
- Use a stick of solder and clean it and borax it before applying it to the joint.
- Heat the work initially with a large, 'bushy' flame, rotating the hearth turntable until the metal strips reach an even, dull red colour. (*Author's note*: if you use bottled gas without a compressor, simply use a large nozzle and concentrate the heat in the required areas after generally heating

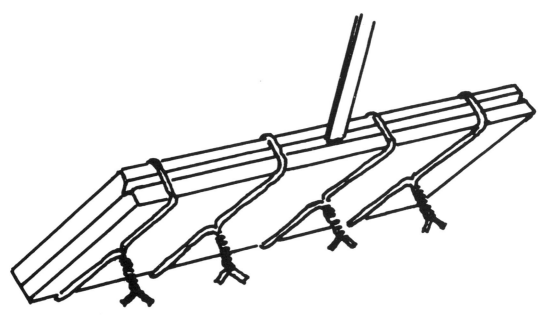

Soldering mokume strips.

Mokume showing solder being pulled through.

the metal to attain a dull red colour.)

- At this point reduce the flame and concentrate the heat on the centre of the block. When the correct temperature is reached feed the stick of solder into the centre, using the angled slot as a way of positioning the solder into the joint.
- Spin the hearth and heat the metal from the opposite side to draw the solder through, to show as a bright molten silver line.
- Spin the hearth again and apply more solder at a point 15mm (0.6in) in from the left-hand end, and spin the hearth yet again to draw the solder through. Repeat the process on the right-hand side and then check that the block is completely soldered. Allow it to cool, remove the binding wire and place the block in the pickle.
- Remove the block from the pickle and file any excess of solder from the surface and add the third laminate of metal, after following exactly the process that was described in the joining of the first two strips.
- Once the three strips have been soldered together to form a block it

should be passed lengthways through rollers until its length has roughly doubled. Remember that the metal will become very hard and you may need to anneal it. You do not want it to delaminate by overstressing it.

- The block may now be cut in two and the halves soldered together, following earlier instructions, thus doubling the number of layers of metal.
- This process may be repeated as many times as is necessary to produce a desired pattern.

PATTERNS

There are two main ways of producing a pattern.

The first is by cutting through the top layers of metal into those below, thus exposing their different colours. This may be done in many ways and the choice is dependent upon the type of pattern that is proposed and the designer's imagination. (*Author's note:* drills, dental burrs, carving tools or files may be used.)

Once the desired pattern has been produced the block can then be rolled into a smooth sheet, eliminating the cuts but displaying the pattern in rings, lines, swirls or whatever was intended. The block will be square and can be first rolled in one direction and then the other in order to retain the shape, or rolled in only one direction to elongate it. Whichever action you take will obviously have a bearing on the final form of the decoration.

It is important not to cut more than a third of the way into the block when you are cutting the pattern, otherwise the sheet may become too thin before it is rolled to a smooth surface.

The second method produces twisted patterns: these normally require many layers, from sixteen to sixty-four, and the final block needs to be made into a square section bar. Once made, one end should be held horizontally in a vice and, gripping the other end with an adjustable spanner, twist the bar as many times as you desire.

(*Author's note: mokume* sheet may be used to make almost anything; the limitation is the ingenuity of the designer. Alistair McCallum has many of his pieces spun, but the author has raised small pieces. For those without rollers it should be possible to forge small pieces of sheet. It really is up to the individual to experiment, since rollers have not always been available. To obtain the full colours in a piece of *mokume gane* it should not be polished but finished with a satin surface.)

14

Finishing and Polishing

Finishing and polishing are extremely important stages in the production of any piece of work. It might be thought that a mere continuation of rather unthinking manual techniques is all that is involved, but nothing could be further from the truth. Poor finishing and polishing can ruin the appearance of a piece, negating its form and ruining its decoration.

Finishing is a term that may be applied to all activities following on from fabrica-tion, construction and soldering. The equipment required includes a selection of files, abrasive stones and abrasive papers. You will need a variety of good quality files and the best are Swiss-made. For working on stakes ordinary engineers' files will suffice. Swiss files are generally available in grades, or cuts, numbered 0, 2 and 4. The most basic set should comprise a hand, or rectangular section, a half-round and a triangular section. Lengths vary from 100

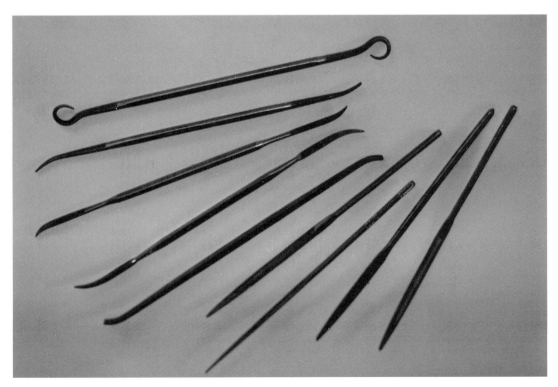

Riffler files.

to 200mm, according to the cut, and also the supplier's range. You will also have to buy handles for your files.

A full set of Swiss needle files is invaluable for working the finer stages of finishing and for working in confined spaces. Riffler files, once again Swiss-made, although expensive, are invaluable for reaching into difficult places, and the author would never be separated from a triangular-section riffler file!

At this stage it is appropriate to consider the actual use of files and rifflers during the finishing process. Their main use, of course, is the cleaning up of soldered joints and it is a stage where great care must be taken. You must always remember that you are removing metal, and rash or careless work will result in a thinning of the metal and may produce hollows or ridges on the surface which will catch the light when it is polished. If you are filing around or along a joint you should not simply file with a straightforward thrust but rather in a combined action, moving forwards and away diagonally from the joint. Do not file outwards any more than you need to do because the file marks will have to be cleaned away in the next stage and there is no point in making work for yourself. Complete the filing by using a fine cut file and a light action, so that you are not attempting to remove very deep marks later in the finishing stage.

You may, if you are not careful, find yourself attempting to finish and polish areas that are almost impossible to reach because of components that were soldered into position at an earlier stage and thus restrict access. It is important to think ahead as you work and, if you can see any difficulties, undertake some finishing and polishing before soldering any awkward components into place. This sort of problem might be avoided at the design stage of some pieces by deciding to bolt components together, so that the several parts may be finished and polished separately. What is quite essential in using a file is that you should work with great concentration and observe carefully the effect of the cutting action at all times. You can view the work from different angles to judge the surface quality and see how the light is reflected. When cleaning a joint with a fine file you should be able to see any traces of solder on the surface, which must be removed. You may also find evidence of an imperfect solder joint in the form of pinholes or a short length of recessed solder. If the blemishes are too deep to remove with the file you must resolder the joint. If a pinhole will not accept solder clean it out with a fine drill and insert a plug of silver wire and reheat it. When you feel that you have gone as far as is necessary, then you are ready to use the next grade of finishing materials.

After using a file, water of Ayr stone and various abrasive papers may be used to produce a surface that is ready for the final finish, be it polish, satin or matt.

Water of Ayr stone, which has been referred to elsewhere, is obtainable in sizes from 3 to 25mm square in section and 10cm long. You should always work with a size that is right in scale for the job in hand. Large, flat surfaces are obviously better worked with a stone 25mm wide and this is the sort of size for stoning a box, always with the lid in place. For general stoning a stick 13mm wide is easy to use. Water of Ayr stone may be shaped to your purpose by using an old, coarse file. It also often needs corners sharpened up because it quickly wears away in use. The actual action of stoning is similar to that of filing, except that the stone is regularly dipped in clean water as it is used. The metal surface must be kept wet in the working area and, to

146

assess progress in removing marks, an old piece of cloth should be available. The stone leaves a matt surface, so that it is possible to see remaining file marks glinting as the metal is moved about. Before stoning and all the other fine finishing processes are undertaken you should clean your bench thoroughly to ensure that there are no filings that could be picked up and rubbed into the surface of your work. You should also regularly change the water which you are using with your stone.

As you stone silver you may be puzzled to see, if you have not already been instructed in it, a distinct colour variation between the area that you have stoned and the area that has not been worked. The area that you have stoned will be white and that that which is unworked a dark shade of grey, and this area is firestained. Standard silver is an alloy comprising 92.5 per cent silver and 7.5 per cent copper, and, when it is heated with a gas torch on an open hearth, the copper in the alloy is oxidized and this oxide builds up on the surface with each heating. The higher the temperature the more the grain structure opens up and the deeper the firestain penetrates.

Firestain can be discouraged at all stages in the production of a piece of work by painting it before heating with a proprietary product *Argo-tect*. It is a fine, white powder which has to be mixed with methylated spirits. It does obscure the surface during heating, but a little practice enables you to judge the heat satisfactorily – but you will, of course, not find unanimity among craftsmen about its use.

If firestain is present on your work it is at the finishing stage that you must decide what you are going to do about it. If you decide to remove it then you are faced with the choice of using fine files, water of Ayr stone or abrasive papers. Obviously, the metal must be thick enough to permit the removal of the stain without a serious weakening and devaluation of the product. Great care will also have to be taken so that fine details and subtle forms are not spoiled.

If you decide that you will retain firestain, or are quite unable to remove it because of fine detail, delicate decoration or planishing marks, there are two avenues open to you. First, you must complete all the necessary finishing and then polish the metal or give it whatever final surface treatment you have decided upon.

The first method involves heating the article with a large, all-enveloping flame until it is just beginning to reach red heat. It should then be allowed to cool before placing it in the pickle for two or three minutes and then washing it thoroughly. This process should be repeated at least six times. Remember that if your work has any hollow components that may retain pickle they must be washed quite clean before reheating. Your work can be boiled in water to achieve this and, if a component has two holes some distance apart, this can help considerably. The author always washes such areas with a syringe, which should be stored securely when not in use. When all the heating has been completed the work should be lightly treated in whatever finish you prefer, using a rouge mop and rouge in the case of a polish.

The second method is to cover the firestain by having the article electroplated with silver. This will give a very white finish, a characteristic of pure silver, but it will eventually wear away.

However, to return to the finishing processes before polishing or whatever final effect you prefer. The use of abrasive papers may be very useful and convenient. Wet papers should always be used with copious quantities of water so as to wash away dislodged grit and to prolong the life of the paper. The most useful grades are those between 800 as a coarse grit and 1200 as the very finest. Dry papers are used for fine finishing purposes, grades 2/0 to 4/0 being the most useful. Abrasive papers may be useful in producing a surface that is finer in texture than that which is made with a stone. These papers may be glued to variously shaped and sized sticks so that they can be used in the same way as a file. They can also be torn into small pieces, folded and used with thumb pressure. Remember to vary your direction of working at all times so as not to make grooves and hollows in your work.

With finishing completed your must consider the final finish to your work, whether it be polish, satin finish or matt.

Most polishing work is carried out by using circular polishing mops which consist of discs of cloth held together by small, central, fibre discs with holes that fit the spindles of a polishing motor. There are three useful grades of mop used by silversmiths, ranging from very fast cutting to one imparting a final polish. The fastest cutting mop is made from calico impregnated with a dressing. It can be used for fast work on silver, but great care must be taken around joints and fine detailing, where grooves or gutters could be cut and detail spoilt and slurred. This type of mop is also ideal for polishing stakes, but you should keep a separate one for this purpose and certainly not use it for working on silver. The second category of mop is also made of calico, but has no dressing and is soft. It is ideal for the early and general polishing of silver and gilding metal. The third category is a fine twill with a soft swansdown pile on one side of each disc of cloth. This mop will produce a very high polish. For general, large works, mops with a diameter of 152mm (6in) are appropriate, while for smaller pieces a diameter of 102mm (4in) may be more suitable. The most useful widths for mops are 25 or 38mm (1 or 1.5in). There are other sizes of mop that, with experience, you may prefer; a silversmith's tool shop will have extensive catalogues. There are also some extremely fine mops consisting of wool or cotton threads, and these are used to produce the very finest polish of all.

Also available for polishing purposes are felt wheels, or bobs, and felt cones. They have a firm surface and should be used with great care because they are fierce in their action.

A polishing medium is required for use with all the mops that have been described. For all preliminary polishing of silver and gilding metal you should use Tripoli, and for following on to produce a high polish you should use radio rouge. To polish stakes and hammers use highfin or crocus.

In addition to polishing equipment there are other products that produce satin or matt finishes and these are essential in finishing the interior of many vessels. There are bristle brushes, known as 'inside brushes', that consist of a central wood or plastic boss, with a hole at one end into which the spindle of the polishing motor fits. All around the boss, including from the rounded end, project long bristles. The brush must be used with a matting medium which may consist of pumice powder and oil mixed to a stiff paste. The mixture becomes runny and hot and is messy in use. Similarly shaped brushes with fine brass wire bristles are obtainable and with these you should use soap or detergent and water as a lubricant. If you use a brass brush without lubricant a dull layer of brass will be deposited on your silver. Alternatively you may use soap-filled pads of fine steel wool, with plenty of water and a light action.

Several well-known silversmiths give the outer surfaces of their work a satin or matt finish. This is a personal matter and it requires some sensitivity to develop a finish that is suitable for your work. A satin finish, probably pioneered by Scandinavian silversmiths, is the simplest to achieve. A fine satin finish is not reflective like a mirror, but if you get very close to it you will just see your reflection. You should first achieve a high polish and then work with a fine wire brass brush with a soap or detergent solution.

If you have concerns about satin and matt finishes you should first experiment on scrap metal so as to gain some confidence.

As already mentioned, there are three grades of polishing mop, and in the first stages of polishing the mop that you will use will really depend upon the finish that your work has. If some hard work has to be done, then you must use a calico mop impregnated with a dressing. In the act of using a mop if you are to avoid damage or disaster there are a few important rules that you must follow. The mop must be revolving towards you and downwards as you face it and you should apply your work at a point below the level of the spindle. To do otherwise is to risk having your work 'grabbed' by the mop and hurled at you. As we have already made clear, if your work is dragged from your hands when you are working correctly you should let it go to hit the bench rather than risk serious injury to your hands in trying to save it. You should apply the Tripoli bar to the mop and then apply your metal. If you are polishing a box, a plate or a lid start polishing in the centre and work down to the edge, never the other way round because the mop will catch the edge, with possible terminal results for your work. You must apply a fair pressure when you work, but not by leaning with extreme bodily pressure, and you should also move your work from side to side so as not to cut grooves or gutters.

After the first polishing you should inspect your work carefully. You will almost certainly find some pinholes in which polishing compound has lodged and which has been dragged out by the mop, leaving a drag mark. You may also find the odd file mark that you were sure you had removed. You must deal with these problems at this stage, going back to water of Ayr stone, polishing papers and even re-soldering if necessary. You simply cannot polish this sort of blemish away and to try to do so will only slur all the detail on your work and ruin its looks.

Polishing to edges is a critical technique as far as the final appearance of a design is concerned. As already described, work down to an edge but make sure that you do not go over it and tend to give it a radius. A critical area is the joint line between a box or any other container and its lid. It is easy to impart a radius to these corners, when in fact the joint should appear as a thin, black line. Stoning, using polishing paper glued to a stick and working with the lid in place are the essential prerequisites in achieving perfection. In fact, you should get as close to a high polish as you can before using a mop, also avoid working across the joint line, but instead go with it.

Preliminary polishing with the fast-cutting mop completed, you can use the untreated calico mop with Tripoli, observing all the recommended safety measures. If your work has a particularly fine finish it is possible to start polishing with this mop.

The final polishing is achieved by using a swansdown mop with radio rouge as the polishing medium. Rouge mops are deceptively soft and gentle, but with too much rouge on the mop they can easily drag your work from your hands, so keep concentrating. In considering what constitutes there being too much rouge on a mop, all mops accumulate polishing compound on their surfaces and traces of metal too. These may scratch your work, particularly when you start polishing with a cold mop. You should, therefore, make a habit of regularly cleaning a turning mop with a steel wire brush or the sharpened handle tang of an old file, moved from side to side.

It remains only to describe two methods of polishing by hand. The first is by using leather; a fine finish should be achieved first, and then, by using leather glued to a stick or held in the hand and using thumb pressure, the work is rubbed over by using Tripoli with *Brasso* as a lubricant. You actually do the polishing with the rough, flesh, side of the leather, not the outer hide, surface. This method produces a soft polish which is kind to decoration and looks good on extremely small items. The other method is burnishing, by using a high quality steel burnisher. It can be useful in reaching awkward areas. The burnisher is passed backwards and forwards over the surface, overlapping each row. A lubricant must be used, such as a soap or detergent solution or your saliva. It is a skilled technique and care must be taken not to leave ridges on the surface. Burnishers may be obtained from a silversmith's tool shop or a print-maker's and etcher's shop.

Reference has earlier been made to the oxidizing or colouring of silver; if it is to be done it must be on the completion of all finishing processes. The most common oxidizing agent is so-called 'liver of sulphur', which is obtainable from a silversmith's tool shop. It is a mixture of potassium polysulphides which will produce a wide range of brown and blacks. It has the smell associated with bad eggs and should be used only in a well-ventilated area. Also available is ammonium hydrosulphide which will produce a bronze colouration of copper. Any chemical that oxidizes metal will be corrosive and therefore dangerous. It must be used with great care and stored securely in airtight containers with clear labels.

The oxidizing agents are used in liquid form and are more effective when dilute, applied in successive treatments if required. In this way a deep colour can be built up. A single, concentrated application gives an uneven coating that often peels away. The metal surface that is to be oxidized must have a matt, satin or scratch-brush finish and be free from grease. If an oxidizing agent is applied to a restricted area, such as a recess in the surface or a textured area, there will occur a fumed overspill on to surrounding areas. Such an overspill can be cleaned away when the oxide has finally established itself in the required areas. Generally an oxidised surface takes a day or so to reach its final depth of colour, so do not be too impatient.

15

Hallmarking

Hallmarking has existed in the United Kingdom for 700 years in a variety of forms, depending upon the date of marking and the place at which the marking took place.

The law which currently governs hallmarking is the Hallmarking Act 1973. The Act makes it illegal for articles of precious metal above a minimum weight to be described as being wholly or partly made of gold, silver or platinum, or to be offered for sale as such unless they carry an approved hallmark.

The details regarding minimum weights and combinations of precious metals are in actuality quite complicated and, if you are contemplating combinations or the production of small objects in very thin metal, you should contact your nearest Assay Office for advice.

The Hallmarking Act was amended as

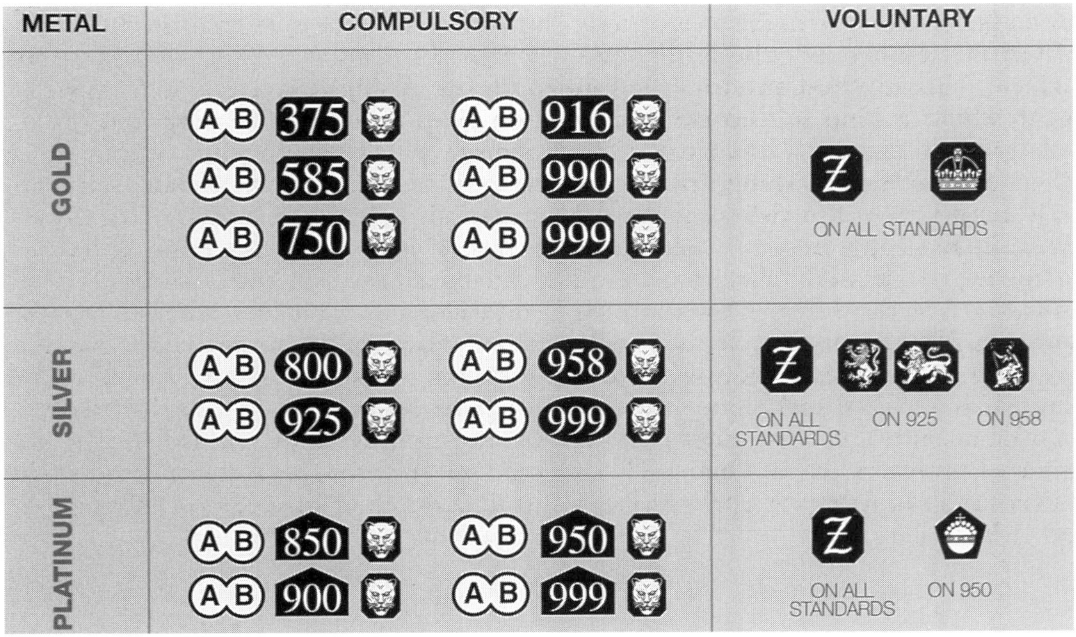

This diagram shows, in the compulsory column, an example of the maker's mark, numbers to represent the quality of the metal and an example of the mark of an assay office, in this case the London leopards head. The voluntary column shows previous compulsory marks which represent the date letter and metal categories and standards. Imported articles will no longer be marked with an import mark.

from 1 January 1999 to bring British law into line with European law. Before that date a hallmark consisted of:

- A sponsor's mark which identifies the manufacturer or maker, importer or distributor.
- A standard mark which usually includes a number and a traditional symbol, indicating the type of metal and its fineness.
- A mark identifying the Assay Office where the article was tested.

Under the amended Act the sponsor's mark, the standard mark and the Office mark remain compulsory.

The accompanying data sheet, which is reproduced by permission of the Assay Offices of the United Kingdom, illustrates simply and graphically the current situation.

Any silversmith may register at the Assay Office of his choice so that his silver and gold may be hallmarked. All Assay Offices operate a personal counter service and a postal service. You should not fully finish and polish your work before presenting it for assay, but you must clean away all surplus solder. The author submits work in a stoned state and takes special care to clean the area where the hallmark will be struck so that it will not be damaged during subsequent work and polishing. The Assay Office has the right to decide where a piece shall be marked, but any reasonable request for marking in a particular position is always considered with sympathy.

A row of punch marks often leaves a raised bump on sheet metal and a corresponding mark underneath. To hammer the hallmark direct will damage the mark but some craftsmen place a piece of soft aluminium sheet over it and use a planishing hammer and stake to smooth the bump away. The author was taught to do the same thing with a piece of lead sheet. If you do use lead always clean the metal well afterwards.

If you wish to register yourself with any Assay Office the addresses of the remaining ones are as follows:

The Assay Office, Goldsmiths' Hall,
Gutter Lane, London EC2V 8AQ

The Assay Office, PO Box 151,
Birmingham B3 1SB

The Assay Office, 137 Portobello Street,
Sheffield 1, South Yorkshire S1 4DS

The Assay Office, Goldsmith's Hall,
24 Broughton Street, Edinburgh EH1 3RH

—— 16 ——

Suppliers

SILVER AND GOLD

J.Blundell & Sons Ltd
199 Wardour Street, London W1V 4JN
telephone: 0171 437 4746
personal counter service; telephone
orders by credit card

Cooksons Precious Metals PLC
43 Hatton Garden, London EC1N 8EE
telephone: 0171 400 6500

Cooksons Precious Metals PLC
59–83 Vittoria Street, Birmingham B1
3NZ
telephone: 0121 200 2120

Cooksons Precious Metals PLC
Unit C, Arundel Gate Court, 1 Froggatt
Lane, Sheffield
telephone: 0114 2419 400
at every Cooksons branch there is a
counter service; telephone orders by
credit card

Thesco
Windsor Street, Sheffield S4
telephone: 0114 272 0966
counter service; telephone orders by
credit card

These firms will also recycle precious
metal scrap and dust.

COPPER AND GILDING METAL

Smiths Metal Centres Ltd
branches in most large cities; telephone
numbers under 'non-ferrous metals' in
the local *Yellow Pages*, otherwise ring
Nottingham 0115 925 4801 for information on your local branch

SILVERSMITHS TOOLS AND EQUIPMENT

J Blundell & Sons Ltd
see under **Silver and Gold**

Sutton Tools
37–38 Frederick Street, Birmingham B1
3HN
telephone: 0121 236 7139
personal shop service; telephone orders;
conditions on request

H.S. Walsh & Sons Ltd
21 Cross Street, Hatton Garden, London
EC1N 8UN
telephone: 0171 242 3711

H.S. Walsh & Sons Ltd
1–2 Warstone Mews, Warstone Lane, Birmingham B18 6JB
telephone: 0121 236 9346
H.S. Walsh offers a shop service and telephone orders; conditions on request

ETCHING SUPPLIES, BOOKS, PAPERS AND OTHER ACCESSORIES

T.E. Lawrence & Son Ltd
117–119 Clerkenwell Road, London EC1R 5BY
telephone: 01273 260 260
personal shop service; telephone orders

Index